D0620648

# A PERSONAL GUIDE
# TO THE UNIVERSE

Nouran Alexander Tawfiq

ISBN 0-9531505-4-2

First published – October 1997
Reprinted – October 1998
Reprinted – November 1999
Reprinted – January 2001
Reprinted – May 2002

Produced for and on behalf of
Universal Star Listing Ltd.

Printed and Bound in Great Britain by
Cox & Wyman Ltd, Reading, Berkshire

# TABLE OF CONTENTS

# PREFACE

My interest in the constellations and mythology started in my early childhood. I distinctly recall being taught how American slaves escaped from the Southern United States to freedom in the North, using only the stars as their guide. As they travelled at night to avoid capture, they would look up and find the "Big Dipper", which pointed to the "North Star". This served as their map to freedom. I was impressed then, as I still am today, by the extraordinary importance stars have held for people throughout history. I found it amazing that people with a different culture, language and history, in another part of the world, could look up in the sky and see exactly the same patterns of stars that I saw. Most exciting, however, were the epic tales of gods and heroes that lay in their background. The Greek myths are filled with stories of bravery, love, jealousy and revenge. As I learned these stories, and began to associate a certain myth with a particular constellation, I was eventually able to look up at the patchwork of the night sky and imagine it as an open book, with each constellation containing a short story.

The purpose of this book is to provide an easy reference to the constellations and their corresponding mythology, or background information. Although there are several excellent books about astronomy and mythology, and some that include both, I was never able to find a book that explained, in layperson's terms, the basic facts about the constellations, with a detailed reference to the mythology behind them. It is that book which I have endeavored to write here.

# INTRODUCTION

We live in a world where the beauty of nature is constantly being eroded by man-made developments. The night sky, however, is one natural wonder which we have been unable to consume. We have all looked up at the stars at one time or another, yet we rarely take the time to understand what it is we are looking at. This book will help you understand some of the basic concepts of astronomy, without suffering its often daunting, technical complexities. Unlike most astronomy guide books, this one is written in simple terms. It is designed for the absolute beginner, and the few technical terms used are accompanied by straightforward explanations. The "Introduction to Astronomy" section features a series of explanations, and defines some of the basic concepts and terms in astronomy. You will not need an array of expensive equipment to see most of the objects mentioned. In fact each constellation can be seen, to some extent, with the naked eye and, only in exceptional cases, are celestial bodies mentioned which cannot be located with a pair of binoculars, or a small telescope.

Each constellation based on mythology contains a summary of its background. The vast majority of these stories come from the familiar Greek legends. One of the most exciting parts of stargazing is learning about the fascinating characters upon which the constellation's names are based. For example, most people probably know that Gemini represents the twins, but how many would know that Gemini is derived from the story of Castor and Pollux, the twin sons of Zeus.

Those constellations that do not have a mythological background were discovered by a handful of European astronomers, between the Sixteenth and Eighteenth Centuries. In these cases, there is a category called "Quick Facts" which explains the constellation's origin. There are also "Visibility" and "Location" sections, detailing where, and when to see each constellation. Finally, each constellation has a "Special Features" section, which outlines their most interesting celestial objects.

With the tools provided for you in the coming chapters, it will not be long before you can look up at the night sky, recognise a constellation, know the name of its brightest star and the mythology behind it.

# AN INTRODUCTION TO ASTRONOMY

The complex nature of astronomy can be a little overwhelming at first. This section is not designed to teach astronomy, but rather to provide some simple explanations of its most fundamental concepts. Once a few of these basic ideas have been grasped, looking up at the night sky will become a far more interesting, and exciting prospect.

## Constellations

A constellation is simply an area of the sky. Like any area, it has a defined boundary, within which lie stars forming certain patterns or shapes. It was these shapes that ancient astronomers likened to mythological gods, heroes and creatures.

## History

The study of astronomy, in one form or another, can be found in almost every ancient civilisation. When the science was first being developed, however, it was greatly influenced, and often obscured by religion. Despite this, the accomplishments of those ancient civilisations, are nothing less than astounding. Their knowledge of the Universe, however, was based solely on the observation of the naked eye. As a result, it took mankind thousands of years to understand even some of the most basic astronomical concepts.

The Greeks, who were highly skilled mathematicians, developed astronomical theories by interpreting their observations. Aristotle (circa 350 BC) argued that the Earth must be round due to the observation that a particular star's altitude in the sky depends upon the latitude on Earth from which it is observed. Thus the angle of altitude on which the North Star (Polaris) appears in the sky, gives the observer's latitude in the Northern hemisphere.

In 150 AD, Ptolemy, the Greek astronomer, drew up a list of 48 constellations. He divided the sky into sections - in essence, casting a "net" around shapes which appeared in certain positions in the sky, at certain times of the year. He divided them into Northern, Southern and Central or Zodiacal (the Greek for "animal"). Each constellation was named after a mythological character, object or animal.

Despite the many amazing achievements of ancient astronomers, the fact that the Earth is not the centre of the Universe took an extremely long time to be accepted. It was the famous Polish astronomer, Copernicus, who first tried to put forth the theory that the Earth orbited the Sun, rather than the opposite. Such a claim was fiercely denounced by the Catholic church. In fact, in the Seventeenth Century, the great Italian mathematician and astronomer, Galileo Galilei, was accused of heresy, and tried by the Church for supporting, and expanding upon, the theory.

Over the centuries that followed, the list of constellations started by Ptolemy was expanded by various astronomers. Navigators and celestial cartographers Nicholas Louis de Lacaille, Pieter Dirksz Keyser & Frederick de Houtman divided the Southern sky that was not visible to Ptolemy. Johannes Hevelius, Gerard Mercator, Petrus Plancius & Amerigo Vespucci filled in the rest of the gaps left between the original 48 constellations.

The whole process was rather arbitrary, hence the unusual shapes and sizes of the 88 constellations we have today. These were adopted in 1933 by the International Astronomical Union, the governing body of astronomy.

**Why constellations move**
Each constellation contains certain stars, which are visible to us, forming some kind of pattern, or shape. When, and if, we can see a particular constellation, depends upon three factors:

1. **The time of night**
2. **The time of year**
3. **The latitude on Earth of the observer.**

## Time of night

The Earth rotates anti-clockwise, completing a full revolution (360∞) in 24 hrs. This gives us night and day. As it rotates, the Sun appears to travel westwards across the sky - rising in the East and setting in the West. It is not the Sun moving, but the Earth rotating that causes this effect. Although we cannot really see the Sun move, a glance from hour to hour will reveal a noticeable difference in the Sun's position. When the Sun goes down, we are able to see the stars. Although they do not appear to do so, the stars actually move very slowly across the sky throughout the night - exactly the same way we watch the Sun travel during the day.

## Time of year

As well as rotating about its axis, the Earth orbits the Sun, completing a revolution every 365_ days. As it does so, our view of the stars at night will change. When the Earth is East of the Sun, it faces the Sun during the day and looks out toward the East at night. Six months later, when the Earth is west of the Sun, it still looks towards the Sun during the day, but faces the West at night. This means that a constellation visible at night in the winter, for example Orion, will actually be invisible in the summer, six months later, because it will appear during daylight hours.

## The latitude on Earth of the observer

What can actually be seen in the sky, depends upon

the observer's position on Earth. For example, someone standing on the North Pole will never be able to see the constellations that are located in the Southern celestial hemisphere, because the Earth gets in the way. However, they will be able to see all of the constellations above, and around, them all year. Contrast this with someone who is standing on the Equator. As the Earth rotates, they will be able to see all the constellations in the Northern and Southern celestial hemispheres, but only at certain times, during the Earth's rotation.

## Celestial hemispheres

Try to picture the Earth as a ball located inside a much larger ball, the Universe. The Earth has a North and South pole, and an imaginary line dividing it into Northern and Southern halves (the Equator). If we project this line, and these points, onto our larger ball (the Universe), we can divide the Universe into Northern and Southern hemispheres with a North and South pole. If an observer was to go to the North pole and look up directly (90∞), they would be looking at the **North celestial pole**. This point is marked (very closely) by a fairly bright star, known as Polaris, or the North Star.

## Star positions or co-ordinates

To pinpoint a particular location on Earth, we can use lines of longitude and latitude. Having divided our Universe into Northern and Southern hemispheres, we can do the same. The celestial equivalent of longitude is known as *Right Ascension* (RA), usually measured in hours, minutes and seconds, and that of latitude is known as *Declination* (D), usually measured in degrees, minutes and seconds. In a manner of speaking, this is an object's astronomical address*. Using these measurements, referred to as telescopic co-ordinates, we can locate any celestial object.

*An object's position changes imperceptibly over time, due to an effect known as precession, which is the wobbling of the Earth in space.*

**Why do stars set?**
This section brings together all of the concepts that we have outlined above. If you were standing on the North pole, you would notice that the stars appear to rotate around a central point - marked approximately by Polaris. All of the stars, or groups of stars (constellations), that you could see, would be visible all of the time. They would never go below the horizon (set). They would never be obscured by the curvature of the Earth, because you are, in a manner of speaking, on top of the Earth.

However, if your vantage point was London, located 51∞N of the Equator, the viewpoint would be different. Certain constellations would be concealed by the Earth as it rotated. They would, effectively, disappear below the horizon, and then rise above it again within a 24 hour period. However, certain Northern constellations that were close to the celestial pole, would appear high in the sky, and never dip below the horizon.

Any constellation that does not set is referred to as being *circumpolar*. Constellations that are visible all year round from Britain, are said to be Northern circumpolar.

## What are Stars?

Stars are actually glowing balls of gas, which can last for billions of years, by creating energy from nuclear reactions within their core. The energy released by stars is massive - despite the fact that we are 93 million miles away from the Sun (which is the star in our solar system), we can still feel its heat.

The stars that we see at night also generate their own energy. However, they are so far away from us that we can't feel their heat. How bright they appear to us, depends upon their distance from us and the amount of light they produce. The important fact to remember is that because a star *appears* brighter, doesn't necessarily mean it gives out more light. It could be that it is much closer to us than another star, that appears dimmer. For example, the star Rigel, in the constellation of Orion is 60,000 times as powerful as our Sun, but very far away from us. Astronomers refer to a star's brightness as its **magnitude\***, which is measured on a decreasing scale. The brighter the star the lower its magnitude. It is generally accepted that we can see stars up to a magnitude of six, with the naked eye.

## Life of a star

Stars "live" for millions of years, and go through a life cycle. They are "born" inside a spinning cloud of gas known as a nebula (the Latin word for cloud). Within a nebula, individual (or double / multiple) stars are formed, which turn their gas into energy (light and heat) and slowly move apart, forming star clusters. A famous example is The Pleiades, or Seven Sisters, located in the constellation of Taurus. Throughout their life, these stars will constantly move away from each other.

The colour of a star will depend upon its surface temperature. Like a naked flame, cooler stars are yellow or red, whilst hotter stars are white or blue-white. Our Sun, of course, is a star. Fortunately, it is quite ordinary, otherwise we might not exist. It is "middle-aged", about 5,000 million years-old, and of average size.

## Star Distances

The distances involved in space are so vast, that they are almost impossible to visualise. These distances are measured in *light years*, which basically refer to the distance travelled by light in one year. Astronomers use light, because at 186,000 miles per second, it is the fastest entity in the Universe. To try to put this into perspective, consider the following :-

The Sun, on average, is 93 million miles from the Earth. Light takes about 8 minutes to travel from the Sun to the Earth. Light takes just 1.25 seconds to travel from the Moon to Earth. Can you imagine how far it is to the Sun if it takes light 8 minutes? Moreover, how long would it take us to get to the next closest star, Alpha Centauri, if it takes light 4.3 years?

## The Moon

The Moon is a large rock, approximately one quarter the size of Earth. The Moon is our satellite, orbiting the Earth each month whilst, like Earth, spinning on its axis. The speed at which the moon rotates is equal to the speed at which it orbits the Earth, meaning that we can only ever see one side of it. Unlike a star, the Moon does not create its own light. The reason that it is so visible to us, is a combination of its proximity to Earth, and that it reflects the light of the Sun.

## The Solar System

The term "Solar System" refers to the Sun and its family, which includes planets, moons, asteroids and comets. The nine planets listed in order of their distance from the Sun are: Mercury, Venus, Earth, Mars, Jupiter, Saturn, Uranus, Neptune & Pluto. The planets are either composed of rock, like the Earth, or gasses, like Jupiter. Whatever their composition, planets do not create their own light, they merely reflect light from the Sun. All the planets, like Earth, orbit the Sun. Accordingly, they will be seen against a different background of stars (constellation), depending on the time of year. The Sun, Earth, and the other planets all lie in the same plane. From the Earth's perspective, the planets keep to a thin band of sky known as the **Zodiac**. The constellations which make up this band of sky are the ones used by astrologers (definitely not to be confused with astronomers) as "signs of the Zodiac".

# LOCATING THE STARS

It is a common misconception that tens of thousands, or even millions of stars can be seen on a particular evening - even on the clearest night, no more than 2,000 stars can be seen *with the naked eye*. This actually makes basic sky navigation much easier, because there aren't too many stars "cluttering up" the picture.

A casual glance at the night sky can be a little bewildering at first. There is no obvious Great Bear (Ursa Major) or Lion (Leo), and to the untrained eye, the stars never seem to make any clear pattern. This problem is really a product of our own expectations - many constellations are easily recognisable once their shape has been identified. Unfortunately, they rarely resemble what they are supposed to represent. In order to spot them you must become familiar with their "real" shape. To help make this clearer, illustrations are provided, showing how each constellation appears to us in the "The Constellations and their Mythology" section.

The main aim of this section is to help you discover that it's actually quite easy to find your way around the night sky. You don't need binoculars or a telescope to take up stargazing. In fact, the narrower field of vision can sometimes be a hindrance. Your only investment will be one of time, and practice.

To the beginner, locating and identifying even the brightest stars can be a daunting task, but there are a few easy tips that will help you along your way. Don't get frustrated if it seems difficult or confusing at first. With a little practice you will surprise yourself. Find an area as far away from bright lights as you can. This is, of course, not always easy in a big city, but you will be amazed at what a difference even a little less light makes.

**Taking the first step**
We begin with an easy exercise, which can be completed at any time of the year in the Northern Hemisphere, provided it is a clear night. All the constellations mentioned in this section are Northern circumpolar, which means that they can be seen all year round. The reason is because they are located close to the *North celestial pole*, and as the Earth rotates daily, these constellations never fall below the horizon in the Northern Hemisphere. The following sections illustrate the most interesting constellations to be seen throughout the year:

**FIGURE ONE** (Ursa Major). Ursa Major is commonly known as the "Plough" or "Big Dipper" and will appear in different parts of the sky, depending on the time of year. Follow the course of Ursa Major throughout the year in the diagram. It is depicted by seven "key" stars.

**FIGURE TWO** (Ursa Minor). Two stars in Ursa Major, Dubhe and Merak, will be used as "pointers" to help us find another constellation. If you draw an imaginary line from Merak to Dubhe and beyond, you will come across another fairly bright star. The star you have located is called Polaris, also known as the North Star. It is located in the constellation of Ursa Minor. Polaris approximately marks the position of the *North celestial pole*.

**FIGURE THREE** (Cassiopeia). Once again, start with Ursa Major, but this time you want to identify the second star in the formation known as Mizar. Once you have identified it, draw a line from Mizar to Polaris, and then continue the line until you get to a slightly imperfect "W" formation of stars. This constellation is known as Cassiopeia. Cassiopeia and Ursa Major are always on opposite sides of Polaris as they rotate around the North celestial pole.

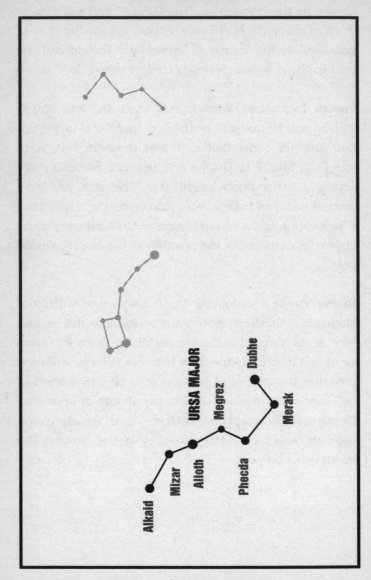

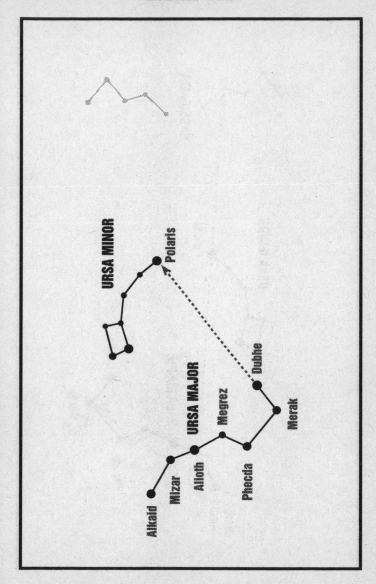

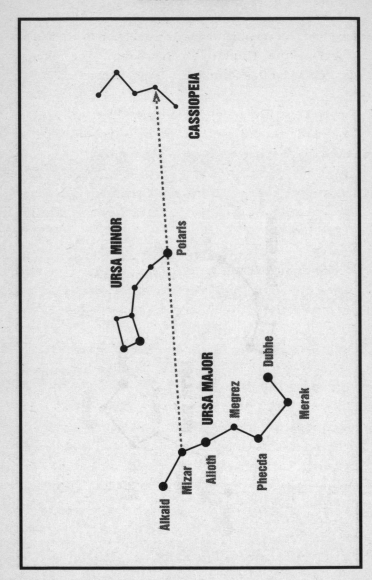

# WINTER

Winter is a great time to view the stars. The nights are long and one very distinctive constellation is on display - Orion, the Hunter. Facing south, the sky is dominated by this formidable, bright constellation.

**FIGURE FOUR** (Ursa Major & Minor). Once again, start by locating Dubhe in Ursa Major and then drawing an imaginary line up to Polaris in Ursa Minor.

**FIGURE FIVE** (Auriga). From there, create a right angle to the next brightest star, as shown in the diagram. This will be Capella, in Auriga.

**FIGURE SIX** (Orion). Extend the line you have created between Polaris and Capella and you will have discovered the most impressive constellation in the sky.

The most distinctive part of the constellation, and the easiest way to recognise it, are the three stars which make up Orion's belt.

The very bright star which represents Orion's right shoulder is Betelgeuse. The slightly smaller star, to its right, represents Orion's left shoulder, and is known as Bellatrix. The very bright star, representing Orion's left foot is Rigel - a star more than 60,000 times as powerful as our Sun.

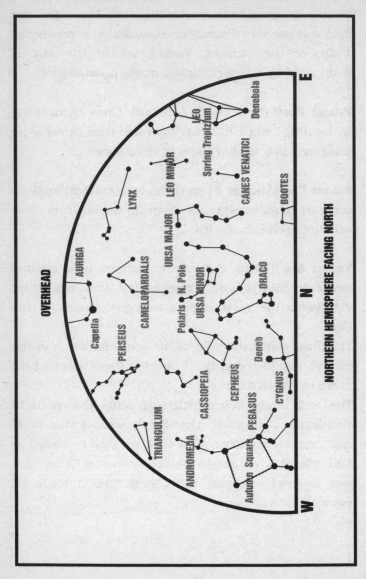

# WINTER SKY (FACING SOUTH)

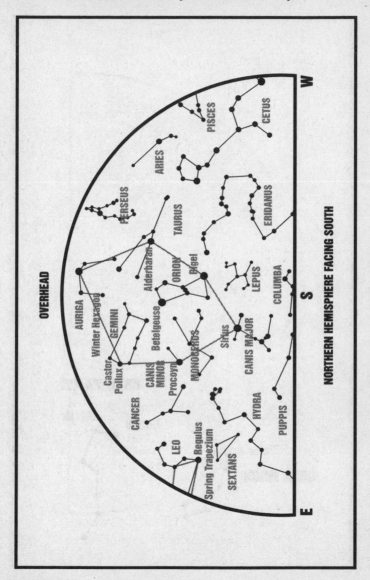

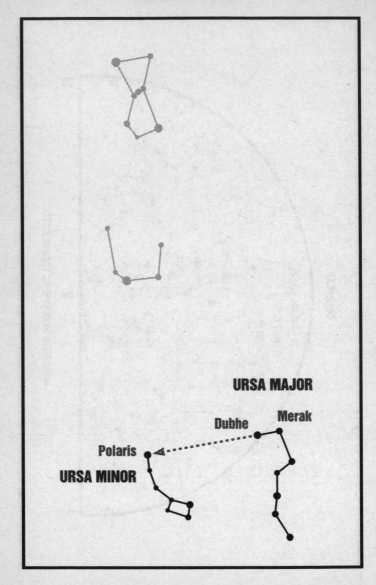

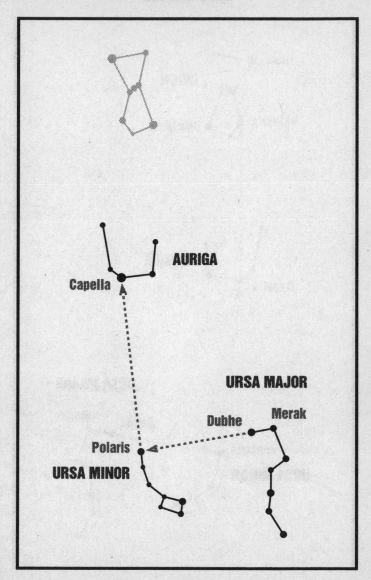

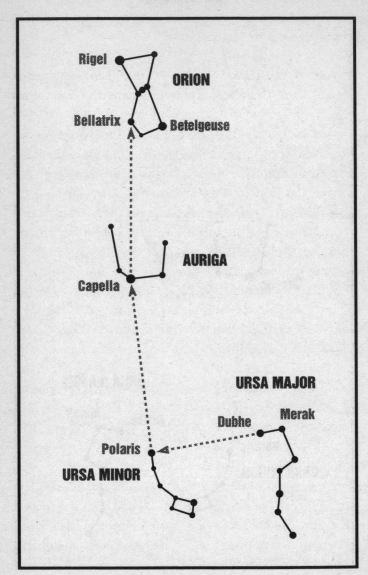

## SPRING

In Spring time, one of the easiest and brightest constellations to find is Leo.

**FIGURE SEVEN** (Ursa Major). To find Leo start, once again, with Ursa Major. First, locate the two stars which make up the bottom of the cup in the "Big Dipper" - Phad and Merak. Follow Phad and Merak downwards and away from Polaris. Extending the lines outwards slightly, you will come upon two stars that mirror the two in Ursa Major but are more widely spread apart. These two stars are part of Leo and using them you can easily locate the two "key stars" in Leo and then decipher the constellation's outline.

Moving diagonally right from the right hand star is a very bright star called Regulus. This marks the start of a curved line of stars, known as "The Sickle", representing the Lion's tail. Diagonally left from the left hand star is another bright star that makes up the Lion's nose, Denebola. Having found these stars, you will be able to distinguish that it makes up the outline of a lion - although it probably more closely resembles a mouse !

**FIGURE EIGHT** (Bootes). Another highly visible constellation in Spring is Bootes. To find Bootes follow the curve of the handle in Ursa Major. You will notice that the final star in the handle known as Alkaid, points to a very bright star. That star is Arcturus and it marks the beginning of Bootes.

To see the rest of Bootes, extend two lines up from Arcturus, and you will notice two smaller stars that are spaced across from each other. Each of these two stars has a partner, which you can find by extending those two lines further again. Finally, take those two lines and join them at the peak of Bootes to complete the outline.

**FIGURE NINE** (Virgo). Having located Arcturus in Bootes (above), extend the curve of the handle in Ursa Major beyond Arcturus until you reach a very bright star called Spica, which is one of the brightest stars in the sky and the brightest star in the constellation of Virgo.

# SPRING SKY (FACING NORTH)

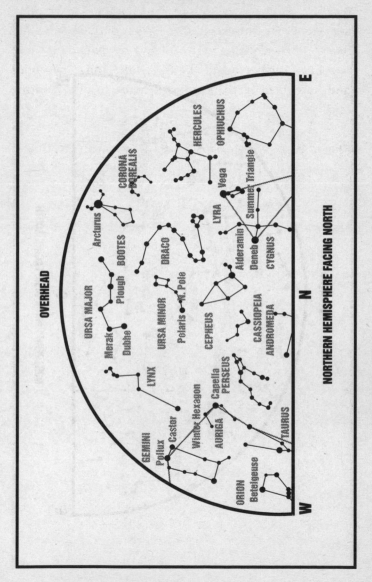

NORTHERN HEMISPHERE FACING NORTH

# SPRING SKY (FACING SOUTH)

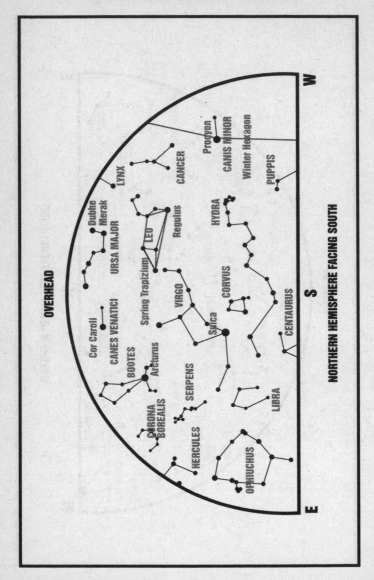

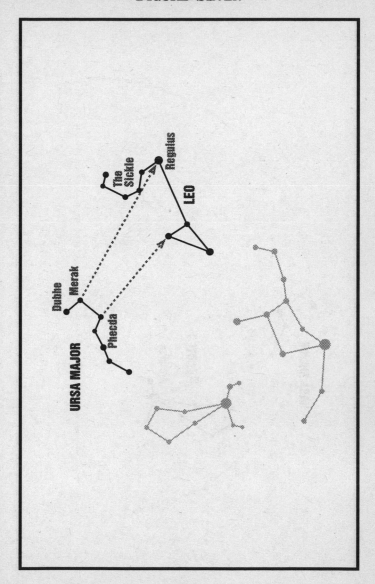

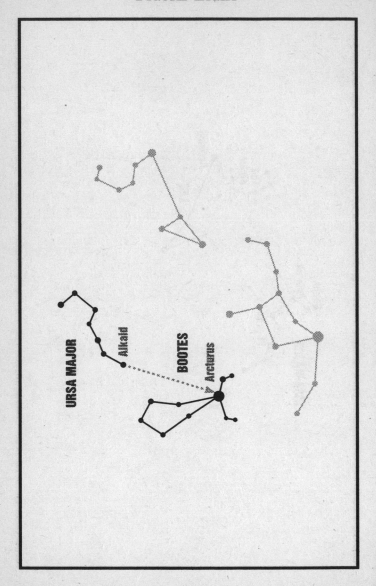

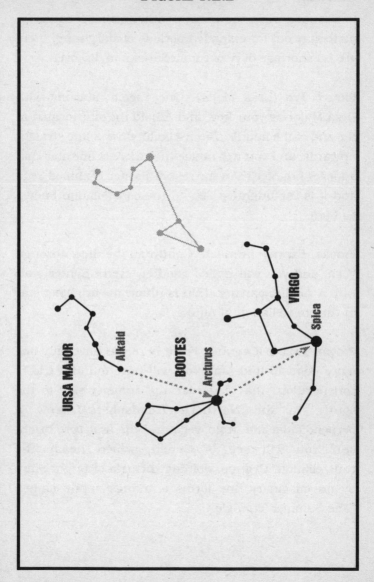

## SUMMER

In summer, when the warm weather makes it easier for us to stay out for extended periods of stargazing, there are no shortage of new constellations to discover :

**FIGURE TEN** (Ursa Major). Once again, starting with Ursa Major as your key, find Alkaid the star located at the end of the handle. From Alkaid, draw a line straight upwards, and you will notice that there is one star that appears brighter than the rest. This star is named Vega and it is the brightest star in the constellation known as Lyra.

**FIGURE ELEVEN** (Aquila). Continue the line through Vega, and you will notice another, even brighter star, with a smaller partner. That is Altair, the brightest star in the constellation of Aquila.

**FIGURE TWELVE** (Cygnus). From here you have only one more point to find, and you will have found a trio of constellations that dominate the summer sky, to the south, in the Northern Hemisphere. Draw a perpendicular line from Vega and the first *very* bright star you will see is Deneb, which heads the constellation, Cygnus. Joining this trio of bright stars by an imaginary line forms a triangle, aptly named "The Summer Triangle".

# SUMMER SKY (FACING NORTH)

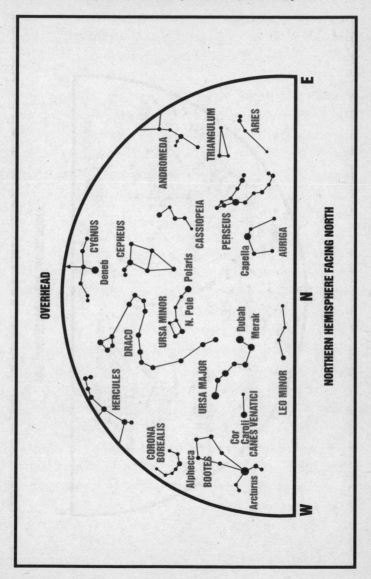

E

OVERHEAD

CYGNUS
Deneb

CEPHEUS

ANDROMEDA

TRIANGULUM

ARIES

CASSIOPEIA

PERSEUS

Capella

AURIGA

N. Pole   Polaris

URSA MINOR

DRACO

HERCULES

CORONA
BOREALIS

Alphecca
BOOTES
Arcturus

Cor
Caroli
CANES VENATICI

URSA MAJOR

Dubah
Merat

LEO MINOR

W

N

NORTHERN HEMISPHERE FACING NORTH

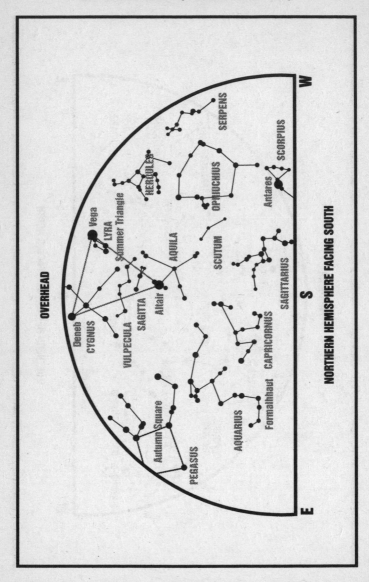

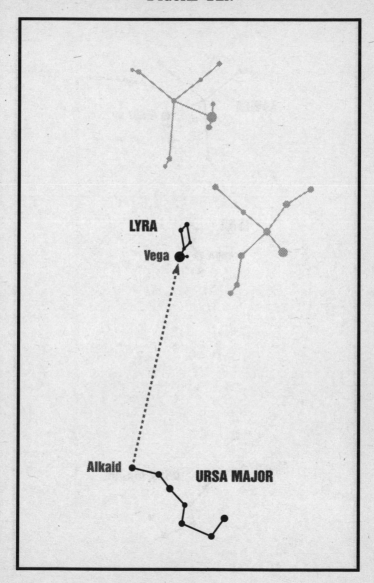

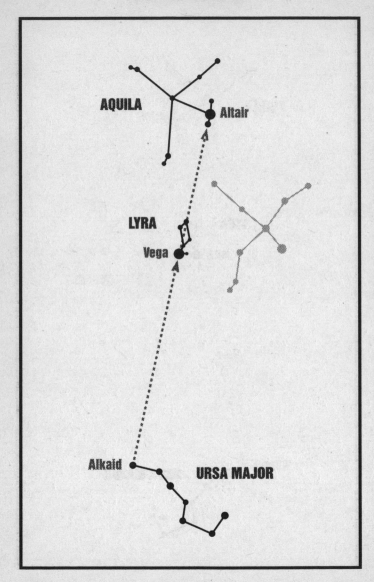

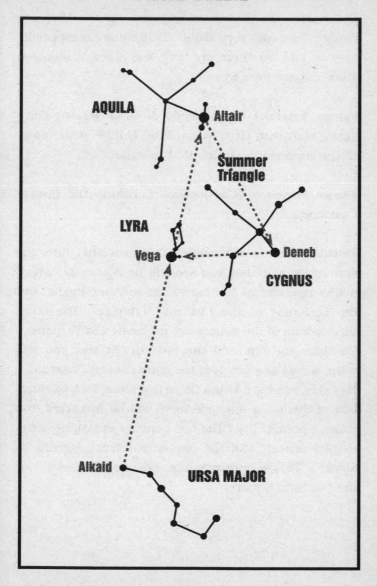

## AUTUMN

In Autumn, the "Square of Pegasus", or the "Autumn Square", becomes very visible. This square is especially easy to find, as there are very few other "naked eye stars" located near by.

**FIGURE THIRTEEN** (Ursa Major & Ursa Minor). Once again, start with Ursa Major. Find Dubhe at the point of The Dipper and stretch that to Polaris.

**FIGURE FOURTEEN** (Cassiopeia). Continue the line to Cassiopeia.

**FIGURE FIFTEEN** (Andromeda). Continue that line, the first bright star that you see will be Alpheratz, which marks one end of the constellation Andromeda, and the beginning of the "Autumn Triangle". The other three points of the square are all located in Pegasus.
Continue the line and the next bright star you will come across is Algenib in the constellation Pegasus.
Now that you have found these two stars, look to either side of them. On one side there will be two stars that make a parallel line. The one across from Alpheratz is named Scheat, and the one across from Algenib, is Markab. This is known as the "Square of Pegasus", or the "Autumn Square".

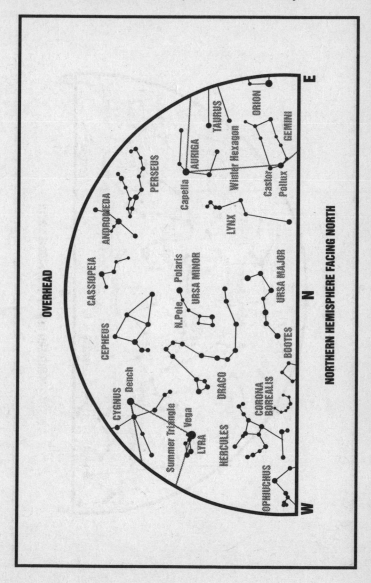

# AUTUMN SKY (FACING SOUTH)

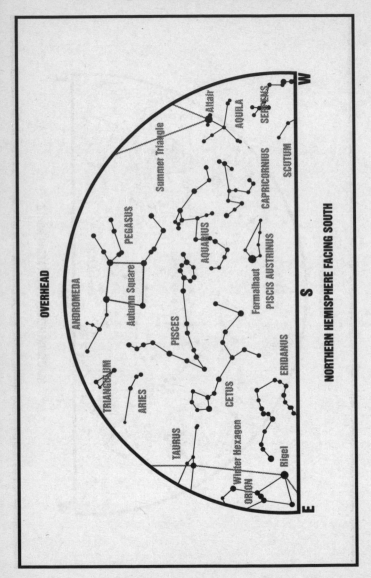

OVERHEAD

ANDROMEDA

PEGASUS

Summer Triangle

Altair

AQUILA

SERPENS

SCUTUM

Autumn Square

AQUARIUS

CAPRICORNUS

Fomalhaut

PISCIS AUSTRINUS

PISCES

TRIANGULUM

ARIES

CETUS

ERIDANUS

TAURUS

Winter Hexagon

ORION

Rigel

W

S

E

NORTHERN HEMISPHERE FACING SOUTH

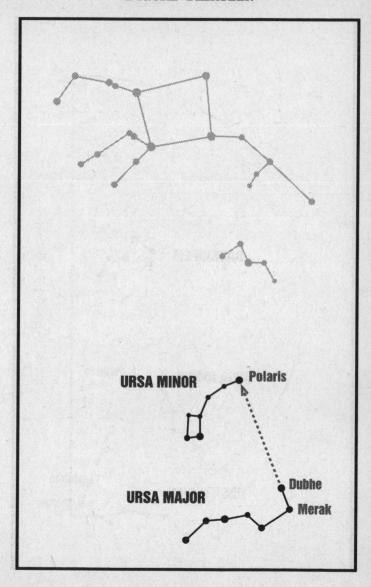

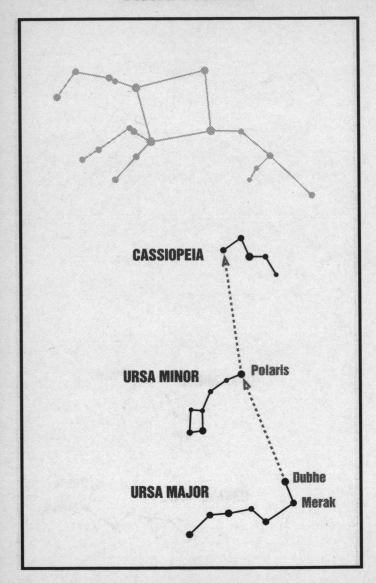

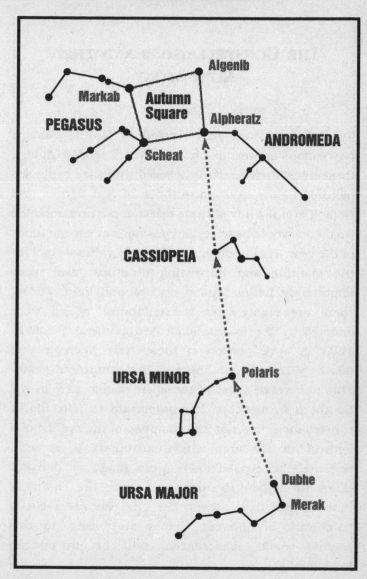

# THE CONSTELLATIONS AND THEIR MYTHOLOGY

Constellations were first created by Middle Eastern civilisations approximately 4,500 years ago. Originally, these ancient civilisations believed that they could see pictures in the sky and outlines of real figures and Gods. Careful study of those celestial pictures revealed that stars would be in certain positions at certain times of the year. This became an extremely valuable tool for the planting and harvesting of crops, and more importantly for navigation on sea and land. Today, there are eighty-eight constellations, which were adopted by the International Astronomical Union in 1933. A large portion of these have been created relatively recently, in the last three hundred years. This is because most of these are visible only in the Southern hemisphere. It is important to note that a constellation does not just comprise of the outline of a figure, but the area which surrounds it as well. Because the constellations were made at different times throughout history, and some are naturally much larger than others, the sky can seem like a patchwork of different shapes and sizes. In this section, each constellation will be introduced individually.

The first part will be the **Mythology/Quick Facts** section which describes the constellation's origin. Most of the ancient constellations, and especially those in the Northern hemisphere, have a corresponding story from Greek mythology. These colourful stories often symbolised in a surreal style, the emotions and practices of every day life. It is easy to forget that Greek mythology was also the basis of religion, and as a result, almost all of the stories have a moral tone to them. Human and in some cases divine, acts of greed, lust, and violence are almost always met with a harsh punishment. Many of these stories have been adopted from other civilisations and incorporated into their own mythology. For example, the Greeks adopted and altered the mythology of the ancient middle-eastern civilisations, to fit their own legends, language and culture. In turn, the Romans did the same with Greek mythology. Eventually, over the course of thousands of years a myth may have scores of different versions, sometimes baring little resemblance to the original story. Because of this, the myths used here are usually the best known versions, and they are abridged to contain the most important aspects.

Those constellations that were named in more modern times, of course, do not have mythology. In these cases, the historical background, such as who they were invented by, and when, is provided. After supplying the mythological or historical background the more practical astronomical information is given.

Each constellation will have a section on:

**Visibility** - when you can see it from Great Britain.

**Location** - which part of the sky is it located in, and which constellations border it.

**Special Features** - a brief summary of some of the most outstanding astronomical objects in the constellation.

# ANDROMEDA - THE PRINCESS

**Mythology:** The myth of Andromeda is part of one of the most enduring tales in Greek mythology, and is linked with those of Perseus, Cassiopeia, Cepheus, and Cetus. As a result of this, their constellations are all located in the same area of the sky. Andromeda was the beautiful daughter of King Cepheus of Jopa (an area in ancient Ethiopia) and Queen Cassiopeia. Cassiopeia, like her daughter, was also very beautiful. Unfortunately for Andromeda, however, her mother's beauty was matched only by her vanity. Cassiopeia claimed that both she and Andromeda were the most attractive women in the world, even more beautiful than the Nereids (Sea nymphs). When the Nereids heard of Cassiopeia's boasts, they complained to Poseidon, and demanded that he defend their honour and avenge her insult. Poseidon (also known as Neptune), who was the God of the Sea, created a great flood that ravaged the kingdom. Then, Poseidon created a fearsome sea-monster named Cetus, to become the scourge of the kingdoms coast. King Cepheus, beside himself with worry over what to do, consulted the Oracle of Amnon for advice.* Cepheus was told that the only way to save his kingdom was to sacrifice his daughter, Andromeda, to the dreaded sea-monster. Devastated by the prophecy, Cepheus begrudgingly ordered his daughter to be chained to a great rock on the coast, while he and Cassiopeia watched the sacrifice from a nearby hill. As the monster was approaching, Perseus, who was one of the great heroes of Greek mythology, was flying overhead (with the aid of his winged sandals). Looking down, he saw the beautiful Andromeda, and instantly fell in love with her. Perseus told Cepheus and Cassiopeia that if they would grant him Andromeda' s hand in marriage, he would save her and kill the sea-monster. Cepheus and Cassiopeia hurriedly agreed to the conditions. Perseus flew down and beheaded the sea-monster with his sickle. Another legend has it that he turned Cetus into a stone, by making him look at the severed head of Medusa (see mythological terms). This stone is said to still be located on the Ethiopian coast. In both legends, Andromeda and Perseus did marry, and returned to Greece where they had a family, but only after overcoming the treacherous efforts of Cassiopeia. For more about the legend, read the summary of Cassiopeia, Cepheus, Cetus, and Perseus.

*The prophecy given by the Oracle of Amnon was typical of Greek mythology in that there was often an ironic truth in it. For example, the only way for Cepheus to save his kingdom *was* in fact to sacrifice his daughter. Cepheus, of course, assumed this was to appease Poseidon or Cetus with a "tribute", but rather, it was to attract the attention of a daring hero.

**Visibility:** All year

**Location:** Andromeda is a Northern Hemisphere constellation bordering Cassiopeia, Lacerta, Pegasus, Pisces, Triangulum and Perseus.

**Special Features:** The most interesting aspect of Andromeda is that it is home to a galaxy that is the twin of our own Milky Way, and although it is located an incredible 2.3 million light years away, it is still visible to the naked eye. This was also the first galaxy outside of the Milky Way to ever be identified. It serves as an interesting and easy starting point for novice stargazers.

## ANTLIA - THE AIR PUMP

**Quick Facts:** Antlia was discovered in 1756 by the French Astronomer Nicholas Louis de Lacaille. It was named in honour of his countryman, Denis Papin, who invented the air pump.

**Visibility:** April - March

**Location:** Antlia is a Southern Hemisphere constellation, which borders Hydra, Centaurus, Vela and Pyxis

**Special Features:** The brightest star is called Antilae, an orange giant with a magnitude of 4.3. There is also an 11th magnitude spiral galaxy, but it cannot be seen with the naked eye.

## APUS - THE BIRD OF PARADISE

**Quick Facts:** This Southern hemisphere constellation was discovered in the late sixteenth century by the Dutchmen Frederick de Houtman and Pieter Dirksz Keyser.

**Visibility:** Not visible in Great Britain

**Location:** Apus is located near the South Pole and borders Octans, Pavo, Ara, Triangulum Australe, Circinus and Musca.

**Special Features:** This constellation, which borders the South Pole, has perhaps the most romantic of names, and also contains some interesting objects to view. Two objects of interest are the double orange giant stars that make up part of the constellation's outline. These stars have a magnitude of 4.7 and 5.3, and although they can be seen with the naked eye, they are best viewed with a telescope as this will allow you to differentiate one star from the other.

## AQUARIUS - THE CUP BEARER

**Mythology:** The constellation of Aquarius is actually based on the Greek myth of Ganymede, the son of King Tros. Ganymede was believed to be the fairest boy on Earth. Because of this unsurpassed beauty, Zeus insisted that he become the cup-bearer to the Gods in Olympus (the home of the Gods). Zeus knew, however, that King Tros would not give his youngest son away willingly, so he disguised himself as an eagle and swooped down to Troy and picked the unsuspecting boy up with his talons. As a result, Ganymede replaced Hebe, the Goddess of Youth, as the server of nectar to the Gods. In order to appease King Tros for the taking of his son, he was assured by Zeus that Ganymede would become an immortal, his image set in the sky forever in the form of the constellation Aquarius. The Egyptian version of Aquarius pre-dates that of the Greeks, and is based on the God of the Nile. Similarly to the Greek legend, Aquarius is a cup bearer. However, he is thought to be pouring the head-waters of the Nile, instead of nectar, to the Gods.

**Visibility:** August - December

**Location:** Aquarius is a Northern Hemisphere constellation, that borders Pegasus, Equuleus, Delphinus, Aquila, Capricornus, Piscis Austrinus, Sculptor and Cetus.

**Special Features:** Aquarius is packed with interesting features. Perhaps the most interesting, however, is the fact that it will be the sight of the famous "Age of Aquarius". This will occur when the vernal equinox moves from Pisces into Aquarius. Unfortunately for those who may be waiting for the "Age of Aquarius", it won't begin for several hundred years.

Aquarius is also home to the famous Helix Nebula. It is the closest nebula to Earth and thus appears as the largest. Although it is possible to see it with the naked eye, it becomes visible in far greater detail with binoculars. The planet Neptune was discovered whilst it passed through Aquarius in 1846, by the German astronomer, Galle.

## AQUILA - THE EAGLE

**Mythology:** There are several legends surrounding Aquila, two of which are represented in the myth of Ganymede (see Aquarius). The first involves Zeus, who wanted to take Ganymede up to Olympus, sending down an eagle to bring him up to the home of the Gods. A second version of this story is that Zeus himself (who often took the form of animals, turned himself into an eagle) swooped down into the Trojan kingdom and brought Ganymede back. Aquila 's claws are known in Babylonian mythology as the symbol of Ninurta, the Babylonian Sun God.

**Visibility:** June - December

**Location:** Aquila is a Northern Hemisphere constellation which borders Sagitta, Hercules, Ophiuchus, Serpens, Scutum, Sagittarius, Capricornus, Aquarius, and Delphinus.

**Special Features:** The most interesting feature in Aquila is the white alpha star, Altair. Known to ancient Arab astronomers as the "flying eagle", Altair has a magnitude of 0.77, and thus is one of the brightest stars in the night sky. Altair is flanked on both sides by Tarazed, a yellow giant star, with a magnitude of 2.7, and Alshain, a yellow star with a magnitude of 3.7, thus making Altair a fairly easy constellations to find.


## Ara - The Altar

**Mythology:** Ara is not shaped in the Western concept of an alter. Instead, it represents a tripod with flames, smoke, or incense, flowing from it. There are several myths that surround the meaning of this constellation, all of them somewhat related. One recounts the epic battle fought between the Titans (see mythological terms) and the Gods of Olympus, before the dawn of man. This was fought to determine who would have control of Heaven and Earth. The battle was, of course, famously won by the Gods. Before going to war however, they swore a sacred oath to one another on Ara the alter. In another legend, Ara is the chasm in the sky in which the Gods threw the Titans after defeating them.

**Visibility:** Not visible in Great Britain.

**Location:** Ara is a Southern Hemisphere constellation, which borders Triangulum Australe, Norma, Scorpius, Corona Australis, Telescopium, Pavo, and Apus.

**Special Features:** One of the nice aspects of Ara is that although, as stated above, it does not outline the shape many of us might imagine, it is nevertheless one of the few constellations in which we can really see the shape that it was named after. As a beginner, this sort of thing always adds to the experience of locating it in the night sky. The most interesting features in Ara are the five separate star clusters, one of which is thought to be the closest globular cluster to Earth.

## ARIES - THE RAM

**Mythology:** The Ram represented in the constellation of Aries is taken from "Jason and the Golden Fleece", one of the most famous stories in Greek mythology. The story of Aries, the magical flying ram with the golden fleece, is actually a precursor to the Greek epic. The original story is about Athamas, King of Boeotia. Athamas is deceived by his jealous second wife, Ino, into thinking he must sacrifice his two children to Zeus or his kingdom will be racked by famine. Zeus looking down on the scene from Olympus was enraged at this deception in his name. To put an end to it he sent Aries his Golden ram down to save Phrixus and Helle. The ram swooped down just as they were to be killed and told the children to jump on his back and hold on. The two children then flew off on the magical ram. Helle fell off and into the ocean but was saved by Poseidon the God of the Sea. Phrixus managed to hold on, and once he landed safely the ram told Phrixus to sacrifice him in the name of Zeus. At first Phrixus refused to kill his saviour, but in the end he understood that this would make the ram immortal, as Zeus would set him amongst the stars as the constellation Aries. Phrixus hung the Golden Fleece in an orchard as a symbol of Zeus' kindness to man. In the Epic tale of "Jason and the Golden Fleece", Jason is sent on a seemingly impossible quest to retrieve the Golden Fleece, in order to win the crown of Thessalian Iolcos.

**Visibility:** August - March

**Location:** Aries is a Northern Hemisphere constellation which borders Triangulum, Pisces, Cetus, Taurus, and Perseus.

**Special Features:** In Ancient Greece, Aries was considered to be one of the most important constellations because it contained the Vernal Equinox. The Vernal Equinox is the point at which the Sun passes the Celestial Equator, and meant the beginning of Spring. This point has since moved on to Pisces and in a few hundred years it will move again into Aquarius, thus marking the dawning of the "Age of Aquarius". Aries has several points of interest, most notably Hamal, a giant yellow star with a magnitude of 2.0, Sheratan, a white star with a magnitude of 2.6, and Mesarthim, a double white star with a magnitude of 4.6. All three are located near each other in an uneven line close to Pisces.

## AURIGA - THE CHARIOTEER

**Mythology:** There are several conflicting myths about the symbolism of Auriga. In one of the more popular myths, Auriga is said to represent Ericthonius, who was one of the original Kings of Athens. Ericthonius' father was Hephaestus, the God of Fire, and his mother was Mother Earth, the living embodiment of the planet in Greek mythology. Athena, the Warrior Goddess, adopted him and brought him up in the holy temple of the Acropolis. Unfortunately for Ericthonius, as a son of Mother Earth he was not completely human. Despite his outward appearance, Ericthonius was a wise and skilled King, with many superhuman talents, the greatest of which was his skill as a charioteer. In fact, he is remembered as the greatest of all charioteers, and is credited with inventing the first four horse chariot. Auriga is also the home of the star Capella, who was the she-goat that mothered Zeus, the King of Gods, in his infancy.

**Visibility:** All year.

**Location:** Auriga is a Northern Hemisphere constellation and borders Perseus, Taurus, Gemini, Lynx, and Camelopardalis.

**Special Features:** Auriga is best known for containing Capella, the sixth brightest star in the sky. Capella, made up of two giant yellow stars, has a magnitude of 0.08, and is easily visible to the naked eye. Capella is flanked by two variable stars. To its left is Menkalinan, made up of two white stars, with a magnitude of 1.9, and to its right is Almaaz, a white supergiant with a magnitude of 3.8.

## BOOTES - THE BEAR DRIVER

**Mythology:** The legend of the bear driver is actually taken from a story about the constellation's brightest star, Arcturus. Zeus had fallen in love with, and managed to seduce, the beautiful nymph Callisto, despite the fact that she had sworn an oath to her companion, Artemis, to never lose her innocence. The product of their union was a son, known as Arcas (Arcturus). When Artemis found out about Callisto' s affair with Zeus she flew into a rage and turned her into a bear (Ursa Major). Zeus then took the baby Arcas and entrusted its care in the hands of Maia, the mother of Hermes (messenger to the Gods). This made him the son of Lycia, and the eventual heir to the throne of the land which would later be named after him, Arcadia.

One day, many years later, while hunting with his two dogs (Canis Venatici), Arcas came across a bear. Tragically, he didn't realise that the bear was his mother, the nymph Callisto. Arcas chased his mother until she hid in a forbidden and sacred temple. The punishment for such a trespass was death. But Zeus couldn't stand to see his son and his former lover killed so he made them immortal by placing them in the sky in the form of Arcturus in the constellation Bootes and Callisto as the constellation Ursa Major.

**Visibility:** February - October.

**Location:** Bootes is a Northern Hemisphere constellation, which borders Draco, Ursa Major, Canes Venatici, Coma Berenices, Virgo, Serpens, Corona Borealis, and Hercules.

**Special Features:** Arcturus is one of the most famous stars in the sky as well as being the fourth brightest with a magnitude of -0.04. This orange supergiant was the first star to be seen during daytime hours, and its distinctive colour can be seen with the naked eye by those with keen vision. Bootes boasts four meteor showers a year, including the most productive of all meteor showers, named Quadrantids. On the 3rd of January every year, you can see up to 100 meteors per hour in the Northern part of Bootes.

## CAELUM - THE CHISEL

**Quick Facts:** Caelum was discovered by the French astronomer Nicholas Louis de Lacaille in the 1750s.

**Visibility:** Not visible from Great Britain.

**Location:** Caelum is a Southern Hemisphere constellation, which borders Columba, Pictor, Dorado, Horologium, Eridanus, and Lepus.

**Special Features:** Caelum is one of the smallest constellations in the sky ranking eighty first out of the eighty eight. The brightest object in the constellation is Alpha Caeli, which is a white star with a magnitude of 4.5. It is neighboured by an almost identical white star, known as Beta Caeli, which has a slightly lower magnitude of 5.1.

## CAMELOPARDALIS - THE GIRAFFE

**Quick Facts:** Camelopardalis was discovered in 1613 by the Dutch Astronomer Petrus Plancius. His religious convictions inspired him to name the constellation after the animal ridden by Rebecca in the Bible.

**Visibility:** All year.

**Location:** Camelopardalis is a Northern Hemisphere constellation which is bordered by Lynx, Auriga, Perseus, Cassiopeia, Cepheus, Ursa Minor, and Draco.

**Special Features:** A fairly large constellation, ranking 18th in size among the 88. The most interesting object for the amateur star gazer is a star cluster located in the middle of the constellation outline. It is visible with binoculars or a small telescope. There are also a series of four double stars located close to the bordering constellations of Perseus and Auriga. The easiest way to find these is by first finding the famous star, Capella, in Auriga, and then looking North by Northeast.


## CANCER - THE CRAB

**Mythology:** Cancer is better known in Greek mythology as Carcinus (Greek for Crayfish). The story of Carcinus is a tribute to the blind courage and loyalty of the tiny creature. It occurred during the mighty struggle between Hercules and Hydra. The second of Hercules legendary twelve labours was to slay Hydra the six headed monster. Hera who raised the monster in order to test Hercules, sent Carcinus, a crab who lived in the Lernaean Marsh, to attack Hercules while he was fighting Hydra. Although Carcinus obviously had no place in a battle between two of the most fierce fighters in Greek mythology, he obeyed Hera, and valiantly tried to aid Hydra in it's battle. Carcinus bit Hercules on the heel, only to be immediately crushed by his powerful foot. Hera put Carcinus in the sky as a reward for her efforts, in the form of Cancer. The constellation is located near Hydra, and at the heel of Hercules in order to commemorate their battle.

**Visibility:** December - June

**Location:** Cancer is a Northern Hemisphere constellation which borders Lynx, Gemini, Canis Minor, Hydra, Leo and Leo Minor.

**Special Features:** Cancer is full of interesting sights for the amateur star gazer. Historically speaking, Cancer was made famous as the sight of the summer solstice better known as the "Tropic of Cancer". In Greek times when the Sun was at its peak (directly overhead on June 21st), it would be located in Cancer. In modern times, the Sun is actually located in Gemini, but the name remains. The most interesting feature is the star cluster known as the "beehive" or the "manger", which is located almost directly in the middle of the constellation. Although it is possible to see the "beehive" with the naked eye, it is clearer with a pair of binoculars. Cancer is also home to a meteor shower, which can be seen around 16 January.

# CANES VENATICI - THE HUNTING DOGS

**Mythology:** Canes Venatici is based in the myth of Arcas (Bootes). Arcas, who was the son of Zeus and Callisto (Ursa Major), was hunting with his dogs in the forest when he came upon a great bear. Unfortunately, he didn't realise that it was actually his mother who had been turned into a bear at the time of his birth. Arcas and his dogs (Canes Venatici) chased Callisto through the forest for miles, until finally she hid in a sacred temple. Arcas and his dogs followed her inside. Any trespass in this temple however, was punishable by death. Zeus was unable to allow his son and former lover to be killed so he put them in the sky as the constellations of Ursa Major and Bootes. The two dogs known as Canes Venatici were not set in the sky and only were reunited with their cohorts in 1687 by the Polish astronomer Johannes Hevelius, when he created the constellation.

**Visibility:** All year

**Location:** Canes Venatici is a Northern constellation neighboured by Ursa Major, Coma Berenices, and Bootes.

**Special Features:** The brightest object in Canes Venatici is clearly the beautiful, white, double, variable star known as Cor Caroli. It is visible to the naked eye and found most easily by looking between Ursa Major and Bootes. The most interesting feature in the constellation is the elegant whirlpool galaxy, which can be seen with binoculars or a small telescope.

## CANIS MAJOR - THE GREAT DOG

**Mythology:** Canis Major represents one of the two dogs that follow at the heels of Orion on his hunting trips and is marked by the brightest star in the sky, Sirius, which is also known as the "Dog Star". It had special significance in ancient mythology because of its prominence. It was even revered as a God in its own right. The great power of Sirius was thought by several cultures to bring the scorching heats of summer. It was a common occurrence, especially during droughts, to offer tributes to the great star in order to pacify it.

**Visibility:** December - April

**Location:** Canis Major is a Northern Hemisphere constellation which borders Monoceros, Puppis, Columba, and Lepus.

**Special Features:** Canis Major is a fantastic constellation, especially for amateur astronomers. It is home to the legendary Sirius, the brightest star in the sky!

Obviously, Sirius is a great starting point for a newcomer to astronomy. You certainly don't need binoculars - it is actually twenty times brighter than Polaris, "the North Star". Sirius is by no means the only interesting sight in Canis Major. There is also the resplendent star cluster, located in the middle of the constellation. Although it can be seen with the naked eye, binoculars are preferable for a real view. There are also three other stars which may pale in comparison to Sirius, but are still very prominent indeed. Adhara, Mirzam and Wezen, all with magnitudes of 2.0, or less can be seen fairly easily with the naked eye.

## CANIS MINOR - THE SMALL DOG

**Mythology:** In one myth, Canis Minor is thought to represent one of the two dogs following at the heels of Orion, the hunter. Another myth is based on Icarius' loyal dog, Maera. Icarius was said to have introduced wine to mankind. While travelling through the countryside, Icarius offered his wine to a group of villagers. As they had never before felt the affects of alcohol, they suspected Icarius of poisoning them. In a drunken panic, they killed the innocent Icarius. His loyal and trusting dog Maera was thrown into despair. Maera refused to leave his masters grave and lay there day and night crying and barking in his grief. Eventually Erigone, Icarius' daughter, was able to find her fathers grave by following Maera' s cries. The image of the dog, Maera, was set in the sky to commemorate his unending loyalty to his master.

**Visibility:** December - May

Location: Canis Minor is a Northern Hemisphere constellation, bordering with Gemini, Orion, Monoceros, Hydra, and Cancer.

**Special Features:** As the name implies, Canis Minor is not quite as impressive as its companion Canis Major, but it still has quite a bit to offer. Most notable is Procyon, a yellow white star with a magnitude of 0.3, which is easily visible to the naked eye. Procyon is Greek for "before the dog", so named because it rises before the brightest star in the sky, Sirius, located in neighbouring Canis Major. Another star of note in Canis Minor is Gomeisa, a blue-white star, with a magnitude of 2.9, also an impressive star visible to the naked eye.

## CAPRICORNUS - THE HORNED GOAT

**Mythology:** There are several legends regarding who the goat symbolises. The Greek legend is that of Capricorn, the God known as Pan. Pan was an anomaly amongst the rest of the Gods. As with almost all Greek myths, Pan's parentage is very questionable. One of the most popular myths is that Hermes, in the guise of a goat, impregnated Penelope. When her son was born, she was horrified to find that his lower half was that of a goat, while his head and torso were human, except for his horns. She abandoned him, but Hermes took him up to Olympus. In Olympus, the Gods were all very fond of him and named him Pan, the Greek word for "all". Unlike the rest of the Gods, Pan had no great ambitions in life except to sleep away his days in the shade of the forest, and seduce as many nymphs as possible during his waking hours. He had no desire to live in Olympus. Rather, he chose the serene life of the woods and streams of Arcadia. When Pan grew to man/goat-hood, he became the object of ridicule to the other Gods, who mocked his lazy nature and simple mind. He is credited with inventing the Pan Flute by cutting reeds of different sizes and tying them together. The greatest of Pan's feats was to turn his bottom half into a fish, and his top half into a goat, in order to escape into a river from the fire breathing monster, Typhon. Zeus was so impressed by this metamorphosis, he set Pan's image in the sky as the constellation of Capricorn. Pan is perhaps most notable for being the only God to die. Despite his death however he has lived on in the legends of several cultures who have incorporated him into their own mythology.

**Visibility:** July - November

**Location:** Capricornus borders Aquila, Sagittarius, Microscopium, and Piscis Australis.

**Special Features:** Capricornus is the smallest of the zodiac constellations and historically, it is associated with the Tropic of Capricorn, the winter solstice when the Sun reaches its Southern most point, on December 22. The Sun now lies in neighbouring Sagittarius for this event, but similarly, to the Tropic of Cancer, the name remains intact in modern times. The most interesting star for amateur astronomers is

Deneb Algedi, a binary star with a magnitude of 2.9. Capricornus is also the scene of two meteor showers occurring, approximately, on the 22nd and 30th of July.

## CARINA - THE KEEL

**Quick Facts:** Carina the Keel was once seen as the keel on the legendary Argonautica, the ship that sailed Jason and the Argonauts through all of their adventures. In 1763, however, the French astronomer Nicholas Louis de Lacaille mapped it as a separate constellation.

**Visibility:** Not visible from Great Britain.

**Location:** Carina borders Puppis, Pictor, Volans, Chameleon, Centaurus, and Musca.

**Special Features:** Carina is absolutely packed with fantastic sights for any stargazer. Not only does it contain Canopus, the second brightest star in the sky, but its location in the Milky Way provides it with a multitude of other sights. Most prominent is the fantastic nebula, located close to the Southern borders of Vela and Centaurus. Close by is a giant and beautiful star cluster, near the borders of Musca and Centaurus, boasting over sixty stars. Both of these celestial bodies can be seen with the naked eye but are well worth a look with a pair of binoculars, or a small telescope, for a true appreciation.

## CASSIOPEIA - THE QUEEN

**Mythology:** Cassiopeia gained her fame as the beautiful mother of Andromeda. Cassiopeia claimed that she and her daughter were more beautiful than the Nereids. The Nereids were Sea-nymphs who lived in the bottom of the Ocean, and were renowned for their beauty and grace. The Nereids, including Poseidon's wife, Amphitrite, complained of this insult and demanded that he defend their honour. He did so by flooding Jopa, and sending Cetus, the Sea-monster, to attack the coast line. King Cepheus, after seeking advice from the Oracle of Amnon as to how to save his kingdom, was told that only if he sacrificed his daughter, Andromeda, to Cetus, would he be able to save his Kingdom. Luckily for Andromeda, Perseus was flying over Jopa on his way back to Greece, and fell in love with her instantly. He flew over to Cassiopeia and Cepheus and made an agreement to save Andromeda, in return for her hand in marriage. Cassiopeia, however, had no intention of allowing her daughter to marry Perseus, especially as she had already promised her daughter's hand to another suitor. Therefore, despite Andromeda' s desire to marry Perseus immediately, Cassiopeia refused to allow it. Perseus foiled her plans by defeating the suitor and his army. Poseidon punished Cassiopeia for her vanity by setting her image in the sky, sitting in a basket that turns upside down at certain times of year.

**Visibility:** All year

**Location:** Cassiopeia is a Northern Hemisphere constellation which borders Cepheus, Lacerta, Andromeda, Perseus, and Camelopardalis.

**Special Features:** Cassiopeia is a great starting point for those just beginning to identify the constellations. It is fairly easy to find, as it is located near Ursa Minor, and forms an easily recognisable "W" in the night sky. The middle of the "W" is marked by a beautiful, blue-white, variable star, known as Cih, which varies in brightness dramatically. Nearby are a series of different star clusters, best seen through binoculars or a small telescope.

## CENTAURUS - THE CENTAUR

**Mythology:** The constellation Centaurus is based on the myth of Chiron the Centaur. Unlike all other centaurs in Greek Mythology, Chiron was very friendly to humans. In fact, he was considered to be the greatest teacher of Gods and men. His pupils included Apollo, Achilles, Jason and Ascalaphus. He taught them the art of medicine, self-defence, hunting, philosophy and music. Chiron was, in fact, one of the most respected characters in all of Greek mythology. One day Hercules was battling some of the other Centaurs when Chiron was caught in the middle. One of Hercules' poison arrows accidentally struck Chiron down. The Centaurs retreated, but Hercules came to his aid. As Chiron was a great doctor, Hercules begged to be told how he could cure him. Unfortunately, there was no cure, because Hercules' arrows had been dipped in Hydras' blood, a fate no one could survive. (see Hydra). Yet Chiron could not die, because he was born an immortal. He was doomed to lie in agony for all eternity. Prometheus, however, was able to turn Chiron into a mortal, thus allowing him to die and escape his pain. Because he was *born* an immortal, he was able to live on in the form of Centaurus.

**Visibility:** Not visible from Great Britain.

**Location:** Centaurus borders Libra, Lupus, Circinus, Musca, Crux, Carina, Vela, Antlia, and Hydra.

**Special Features:** Centaurus is a favourite constellation for many, because it has the rare quality of actually looking quite like the myth it was named after. It may take some time to put the pieces together, but with a little perseverance, it will appear. Without doubt, the starting point should be Alpha Centauri, the third brightest star in the sky. Made up of two yellow stars, it has an incredible magnitude of -0.27. Alpha Centauri represents one of the front hooves of the centaur. Parallel to it is Hadar, an extremely bright, blue, giant star, with a magnitude of 0.6. Agadar represents the Centaur's other front hoof . Just work your way up from there, and soon you will be able to see one of the more impressive constellations in the sky.

## CEPHEUS - THE KING

**Mythology:** Cepheus was the King of Jopa, which he ruled with his beautiful wife, Cassiopeia, and his equally beautiful daughter, Andromeda. Cepheus' wife Cassiopeia was terribly vain, so much so that she once boasted that she and Andromeda were more beautiful than the Nereids, who were sea nymphs, renowned for their beauty and grace. The Nereids complained of this insult to Poseidon and demanded that he punish Cepheus and his conceited wife. Poseidon sent a terrible flood to Jopa, and then unleashed Cetus the Sea-monster to ravage Jopa's coast. Cepheus was powerless as his kingdom and his subjects were being destroyed. He went to the Oracle of Amnon to seek advice. The Oracle prophesied that the only way to save his kingdom was to sacrifice his daughter Andromeda to the sea-monster. Cepheus was beside himself with despair. He couldn't willingly allow his daughter to be killed, yet, if he didn't, his kingdom and all of its inhabitants would be destroyed. In the end, Cepheus succumbed to the good of the many and ordered his daughter to be chained to a great rock on the coast. Just when the monster was approaching Andromeda, Perseus was flying above the spectacle and offered to kill the monster in exchange for Andromeda's hand in marriage. Cepheus quickly agreed to the terms and Perseus flew down with the aid of his winged sandals and beheaded the beast. Thus, saving not only his future wife, but Cepheus and his kingdom.

**Visibility:** All year

**Location:** Cepheus is bordered by Cassiopeia, Lacerta, Cygnus, Draco Ursa Minor, and Camelopardalis.

**Special Features:** Cepheus has a significant number of interesting objects. One of the best things about Cepheus for the novice is that its proximity to Polaris makes it fairly easy to find. The best star to look at in Cepheus is Alderamin. With a magnitude of 2.4, this white star is fairly easy to find. About a third of the distance between Alderamin and Polaris ( the North Star) is Alfirk, a variable, and double star.


# CETUS - THE WHALE

**Mythology:** Cetus is linked with the story of Perseus, Andromeda, Cassiopeia and Cepheus. In Greek mythology, Cetus was a giant Sea-monster, who was a subject of Poseidon, King of the sea. When Cassiopeia, the Queen of Jopa, boasted that she and her daughter,

Andromeda, were more beautiful than the Nereids(Sea-nymphs) they complained to their protector Poseidon. Poseidon, who was enraged by the insult, sent Cetus to attack the coast line of Jopa. Cetus continued to ravage the country, until King Cepheus was forced to consult the Oracle at Amnon, which told him that he must sacrifice his daughter, Andromeda, to Cetus. Just as Cetus was approaching Andromeda, he was slain by Perseus, who saved and eventually married her.

**Visibility:** September - February

**Location:** Cetus is a Northern hemisphere constellation, which borders Aries, Pisces, Aquarius, Sculptor, Fornax, Eridanus and Taurus.

**Special Features:** Cetus is a huge constellation, ranking fourth largest in the sky. The brightest star in the constellation is Deneb Kaitos, a giant yellow star, with a magnitude of 2.0. Deneb Kaitos, however, is not the most famous star. That honour belongs to Omicron Ceti, a red giant variable star, which was the first variable star to be discovered and fluctuates amazingly from ninth to third magnitude over a period of 332 days.

## CHAMAELEON - THE CHAMELEON

**Quick Facts:** Chamaeleon was discovered towards the end of the 16th century by Frederick de Houtman and Pieter Dirkszoon Keyser.

**Visibility:** Not visible from Great Britain.

**Location:** Chameleon is Southern circumpolar and

borders Carina, Volans, Mensa, Octans, Apus, and Musca.

**Special Features:** In keeping with its name, Chameleon is rather hard to detect. The long, thin diamond shape, that makes up the outline of the constellation is located extremely close to the celestial South pole. The five stars that account for the outline are all between magnitudes of 4 and 6. The only point of real interest in Chameleon is a planetary nebula, located on the Southern side of the diamond. It is necessary however, to have a fairly powerful telescope to make it out.

## CIRCINUS - THE COMPASSES

**Quick Facts:** This tiny Southern Hemisphere constellation was discovered in 1756 by the French astronomer Nicholas Louis de Lacaille.

**Visibility:** Not visible form Great Britain

**Location:** Circinus is located in the Southern Hemisphere and borders Norma, Lupus, Centaurus, Crux, Musca, Apus, and Triangulum Australe.

**Special Features:** Circinus is a long, thin triangle in the Southern sky. Interestingly, two of the three points in the triangle are made up of double stars, but apart from that, there is not a great deal to look at in what is one of the tiniest constellations in the sky. Circinus is surprisingly easy to find, despite its size, because it is located to the South west of Alpha Centauri, the third brightest star in the sky.

## COLUMBA - THE DOVE

**Mythology:** The legend on which the constellation Columba is based is fairly obscure. It comes from the story of Jason and the Argonauts. As the Argonauts were approaching the dreaded Clashing Rocks of Symplegades, Euphemus caught a dove, which he held trembling in his hands. The waves started to crash all about them, and they became filled with the fear of death. Euphemus let the dove go and all of the Argonauts watched it fly through the rocks, showing them a passage through. This sight gave the Argonauts courage, and they came through alive thanks not only to the dove but more importantly to the help of the Goddess Athena, who blew the ship through the rocks. None the less, the Dove was put in the sky by Athena to commemorate its role in saving the lives of the Argonauts.

**Visibility:** January and February.

**Location:** Columba is a Southern Hemisphere constellation bordering Lepus, Caelum, Pictor, Puppis and Canis Major.

**Special Features:** Columba is an aesthetically pleasing, if somewhat faint constellation. Although there is not a great deal for the novice astronomer, it is possible to see the outline of the doves out stretched wings as it flies, if not through the clashing rocks, then through neighbouring Sirius and Canopus, the two brightest stars in the sky.

## COMA BERENICES - BERENICES HAIR

**Mythology:** Coma Berenices is based on the story of the Egyptian Queen Berenice, who was so worried about her husband King Ptolemy III going into battle, that she cut off her beautiful flowing hair as an offering to the Gods, so that he would return home alive. The Gods accepted her sacrifice, and delivered King Ptolemy from battle safe and victorious.

**Visibility:** All year.

**Location:** Coma Berenices is a Northern Hemisphere constellation which borders Canes Venatici, Ursa Major, Leo, Virgo, and Bootes.

**Special Features:** The outline of Coma Berenices forms what in astronomy is fairly rare, the perfect symmetry of perpendicular lines. This symmetry is complimented by the incongruent array of stars (the Coma Star Cluster), forming the third side of the triangle. With a little imagination, you can imagine Queen Berenice's flowing hair.

## CORONA AUSTRALIS - THE SOUTHERN CROWN

**Mythology:** Corona Australis is based on the story of Dionysus saving his mother from the Underworld. Dionysus was the product of a union between his mother Semele, and Zeus. Semele was a mortal and, of course, Zeus was King of the Gods. When Zeus seduced mortals, he would not reveal himself in his natural form, but Semele who was in love with Zeus, begged him to reveal his true image to her. Zeus agreed, but when he did so, she was struck dead by one of the lightning bolts that surrounded him. Zeus quickly cut the unborn Dionysus out of her womb, and put him in his own leg, where he was eventually "born again". When Dionysus grew to be a god himself, he swore that he would find the mother he had never known. Dionysus went into the Underworld and after working out an exchange of the myrtle plant for his mother, he guided her out of the Underworld and back to life. When she was restored to life in the natural world, Dionysus threw his crown into the sky to celebrate their reunion, where it stayed. That crown is known today as Corona Australis, or the Southern Crown.

**Visibility:** Not visible from Great Britain.

**Location:** Corona Australis is a Southern Hemisphere constellation which borders Sagittarius, Scorpius, Ara, and Telescopium,

**Special Features:** The Southern Crown closely mirrors the Northern crown, but lacks the symmetry and brightness of Corona Borealis. Still, it is not to difficult to make out the crown, especially with a pair of binoculars, or a small telescope. The most interesting feature is a globular cluster, located in the South-east corner of the constellation. There is a meteor shower known as Corona Australids, that can be seen on the 16th of March.

## CORONA BOREALIS - THE NORTHERN CROWN

**Mythology:** Corona Borealis is one of the most geometrically perfect constellations, as well as the one that resembles most the myth which it is based on. The Greeks thought that the constellation looked like a crown, and the myth is based upon the story of Theseus, Prince of Athens, and one of the greatest Greek heroes. Unfortunately for Theseus, and his fellow Athenians, Athens was under the control of Crete. Once a year the Athenians were forced to sacrifice their fourteen most beautiful young men and women to the Minotaur, who lived in a giant labyrinth in Crete. The Minotaur was a horrible and brutal beast, with the body of a human and the head of a bull. Theseus vowed to put an end to this savagery, and offered himself as one of the sacrifices, in hope of killing the Minotaur. When he arrived in Crete, the beautiful Princess Ariadne fell in love with him at first sight. She could not bare to see him slain by the Minotaur, so she secretly supplied him with a sword and a spool of thread.

She told Theseus to let the string out behind him, so that he could find his way out of the labyrinth. Theseus slew the monster and managed to escape with Ariadne to a deserted island. In fact, the island was not deserted, it belonged to Bacchus, the God of Vine. Once Ariadne fell asleep, Theseus sailed away, and left her forever. The next morning Bacchus came upon the heartbroken princess, and fell madly in love with her. He begged her to marry him, but Ariadne had, had enough of men. Bacchus explained to her that he was no man, but in fact a great and powerful god. In order to prove it, he took his crown, and threw it into the sky, and there it stayed as Corona Borealis. He told Ariadne that the crown would be her wedding present, forever hailing her beauty to God and Man.

**Visibility:** February - October.

**Location:** Corona Borealis is a Northern Hemisphere constellation which borders Bootes, Serpens, Hercules, and Draco.

**Special Features:** The Northern Crown is a beautiful and aptly named constellation. What it lacks in celestial objects it makes up for in its shape. The most alluring feature is its crowning jewel, although it is not directly in the middle of the crown. The blue-white variable star, known as Gemma, has a magnitude of 2.2, which is an impressive sight, even with the naked eye.

## CORVUS - THE CROW & CRATER - THE CUP

**Mythology:** The story of Corvus the crow is linked with that of the constellation Crater the Cup. Legend has it that Apollo the God of music, poetry, and beauty was thirsty, and sent his trusted crow to fetch him a cup of water from a legendary fountain. The raven took the cup in his beak, and immediately flew off to the fountain. When he arrived, he saw that there was a fig tree, whose fruit had not quite ripened yet. The crow could not resist, and rested in the luxurious shade of the tree, while waiting for the figs to ripen. After a few days they were perfect, and he gorged himself. Corvus realised that Apollo would be angry that he had not returned. So, spotting a water snake, he grabbed it with his beak and carried the water back in his claws. When Corvus saw Apollo, he explained that the snake had attacked him and he bravely had fought it off, which accounted for his delay. Apollo knew that the raven was lying, and in his anger, threw the crow and the cup into the sky, creating the constellations of Corvus and Crater. As added punishment for the crow's greed his constellation is forever chasing the cup through the sky, never being able to catch it and quench his thirst.

**Visibility:** February - June

**Location:** Corvus is a Northern Hemisphere constellation which borders Virgo Crater, Hydra, and Centaurus.

**Special Features:** Corvus is a simple constellation composed mostly of the six stars which make up its outline. The most interesting of these objects is Kraz, a yellow giant star with a magnitude of 2.7, and Gienah (located directly across from it), a giant blue white star with a magnitude of 2.6.

## CRATER

**Visibility:** March - June

**Location:** Crater is located near the ecliptic and is bordered by Virgo, Leo, Sextans, Hydra, and Corvus.

**Special Features:** Crater is a medium sized constellation whose shape appears more like an ancient chalice than what we think of today as a cup. Its brightest feature is a giant orange star, with a magnitude of 3.6. The only star in the sky that was named in ancient times is Alkes, a yellow giant star, with a magnitude of 4.1.

## CRUX - THE CROSS

**Quick Facts::** Crux, also known as The Southern Cross, was first identified by Western observers in the 16th Century. Although it is a fairly small constellation, its perfect symmetry makes it appear like the Christian symbol. It is easily recognisable, and it is held in the same esteem in the Southern Hemisphere as is the "Plough" is for us in the Northern Hemisphere.

**Visibility:** Not visible in Great Britain.

**Location:** Crux is a Southern Hemisphere constellation, which borders Musca, and Centaurus.

**Special Features:** The Southern Cross is one of the most famous of all constellations, despite its location so far South. It is the equivalent of Ursa Minor and the North Star to the peoples of the Southern Hemisphere. The brightness, and near perfect form of the cross, has become a welcome sight for sailors and navigators in the Southern seas. It is also one of the most beautiful and fascinating constellations, despite its relatively tiny stature. Most notably, it is home to the famous "Coal Sack Nebula". This giant nebula not only covers a large portion of Crux, but stretches into the neighbouring constellations of Musca and Centaurus. Another treasure of Crux is the star cluster known as the Jewel Box. This cluster is visible to the naked eye and is host to an array of different coloured stars.

# CYGNUS - THE SWAN

**Mythology:** There are several myths behind Cygnus the swan. One is that it represents the form Zeus took in order to seduce Leda, the wife of King Tyndareus. A more popular one concerns Helios, Phaethon and Cygnus. Phaethon was the illegitimate son of Helios (The Sun God), but he only learned of this when he was a teenager. He told all of his friends, but none believed him. Phaethon knew that he must confront his father and prove his lineage. When he did, Helios proudly admitted that he, indeed, was his father and offered him any favour in order to prove this. Without hesitation, Phaethon, asked to ride Helios' chariot across the sky, as he did every evening. Helios begged his son to choose something else, as it was far too dangerous for anyone but himself. Phaethon accused his father of breaking his word, and forced him to concede the reins of his chariot. Phaethon took to the sky, and was immediately out of control, veering away from Draco the Dragon, Scorpius the scorpion and all the rest of the constellations. He then lost consciousness, suddenly plummeting to Earth. Zeus and Helios looked on in horror, and Zeus was forced to strike Phaethon down with a lightning bolt, as he was in danger of destroying the Earth. Phaethon's body fell into the river Eridanus, where his grief stricken friend, Cygnus, dove to recover him. Cygnus was too late to save him, but he continued to dive into the water and retrieve the body in order to give him a proper burial. The Gods looked down at the sight of Cygnus gracefully diving over and over into the river, and they all agreed he looked like a swan. In commemoration of Cygnus' love for his friend, Zeus set the image of the swan in the sky.

**Visibility:** All year.

**Location:** Cygnus is a Northern Hemisphere constellation, which borders Draco, Lyra, Vulpecula, Pegasus, Lacerta, and Cepheus.

**Special Features:** Cygnus, also known as the "North Cross", is a fascinating constellation. Located in the Milky Way, it has a wide variety of celestial objects, several of which are visible with the naked eye or with a pair of binoculars. Deneb, a blue-white super giant, is the most famous star in the constellation, with a magnitude of 1.3. More remarkable, but less luminous, is Albireo, a double star consisting of one blue-green and one yellow star. Cygnus is also home to two famous nebulas- the "North America Nebula" and a blinking planetary nebula in the Southern part of the constellation near the border of Vulpecula. Cygnus is also home to a meteor shower on the 18th of August.

# DELPHINUS - THE DOLPHIN

**Mythology:** The constellation Delphinus is based on the story of the Corinthian musician Arion, who was known as the greatest harpist in Greece. His reputation carried him all over the world to entertain royalty. Arion had played on the island of Crete where he so impressed his audience, they showered him with gold and jewels. When he was sailing back to Corinth, the crew of the ship realised that they could quite easily kill him and steal his riches, while blaming his disappearance on an accident at sea. Arion overheard their plans, and, realising he was doomed, begged to play his harp once more before he died, promising to then throw himself into the sea. When Arion began to play, he did so more exquisitely than he had ever done before. All of the creatures in the sea rose to the surface to hear his song. When Arion was finished, he threw himself into the sea. One of Poseidon's dolphins immediately came to his rescue and carried him back to Corinth. Meanwhile, the murderous crew of the ship arrived after him and went to the Corinthian King to explain the tragic death of Arion. Arion, however, was already there, and the King sentenced the crew to death. Poseidon set the image of the dolphin in the sky for saving Arion 's life.

**Visibility:** June - December

**Location:** Delphinus is a Northern Hemisphere constellation, which borders Equueleus, Pegasus, Cygnus, Sagitta, and Aquila.

**Special Features:** Delphinus is a small, but elegant, constellation, whose precise outline does somewhat accurately portray its namesake. The most brilliant star in the constellation is Sualocin, a blue-white star with a magnitude of 3.8.


# DORADO - THE SWORDFISH

**Quick Facts:** Frederick de Houtman and Pieter Dirkszoon identified Dorado in the late 16th Century.

**Visibility:** Not visible in Great Britain.

**Location:** Dorado is a Southern Hemisphere constellation, which borders Caelum, Horologium, Reticulum, Mensa, Volans, and Pictor.

**Special Features:** Dorado is packed with interesting features, one of which is the "Tarantula Nebula". It is the largest nebula in the sky, and takes up a large part of the Southernmost quarter of Dorado, as well as some of neighbouring Mensa. Dorado is also home to one of the largest supernovas ever recorded.

## DRACO - THE DRAGON

**Mythology:** The Dragon is one of the most popular characters in the mythologies of several cultures. For this reason, there are scores of legends that claim to represent the constellation of Draco The Dragon. One dates back to before the time of the Gods, when the world was ruled by a group of giants (Titans) and monsters, one of which was Draco the Dragon. The Gods went to war with the Titans, and Athena the Goddess of War went into battle with Draco. She managed to grab him by his tail and swung the dragon around until she finally let go, and it flew into the heavens, where it sleeps to this day as the constellation of Draco. Another, better known, myth is that of Hercules and his final labour. He was ordered to steal one of the golden apples of the Hesperides. These apples were grown on a tree that was a wedding present to Hera. As the tree bore golden fruit, it was clearly a great prize of thieves, so Hera had it planted in a secret garden near mount Olympus. She had three nymphs, known as the Hesperides guard, and tend to it. She also had a great dragon coil its reptilian body around the tree, so no one would dare try to steal, or even approach the tree. There are two myths about how Hercules stole the apples. One was that he crept up on the dragon, who had grown lazy, as no one ever dared approach, and chopped off his head. Another is that he fooled Atlas, whose job it was to hold up the sky, into getting the apples for him, while Hercules held up the sky in his absence. When Atlas returned with the apples he offered to take them back for him as well. Hercules knew that this was a ruse, so he agreed to it, if Atlas would hold up the sky while Hercules shifted into a more comfortable position. As soon as Atlas did this Hercules hurried off with the apples, leaving Atlas to his rather unenviable task for all eternity. What ever the case, Hera, in her anger at the Dragon, placed him in the sky as punishment for allowing her enemy Hercules to defeat him.

**Visibility:** All year.

**Location:** Draco is a Northern Hemisphere constellation which borders Cepheus, Cygnus, Lyra, Hercules, Bootes, Ursa Major and Camelopardalis.

**Special Features:** Draco is a gigantic constellation that almost completely surrounds Ursa Minor. In fact, its most impressive star, Thuban, was once the pole star thousands of years ago. This title, of course, passed over to Polaris now, as a result of precession (see astronomical terms). The brightest star in the constellation fittingly lies in the Dragon's head, and is named Eltanin. It is an orange giant with a magnitude of 2.2. Draco is the home to three meteor showers, falling on the 28th of January, the 16th of July, and 9th of October.

## EQUULEUS - THE LITTLE HORSE

**Quick Facts:** Despite the fact that this constellation was discovered by the famous Greek astronomer, Ptolemy, there is no corresponding mythology. Equuleus may have been over looked in this regard because of its size. It is the second smallest constellation in the sky.

**Visibility:** July - December.

**Location:** Equuleus is a Northern Hemisphere constellation, which borders with Delphinus. Aquila, Aquarius, and Pegasus.

**Special Features:** Equueleus is a tiny, and ancient constellation, but it still has an interesting and peculiar aspect. One of its stars, known as 1 Equ, is a triple star that is constantly orbiting itself. Unfortunately, this cannot be seen with the naked eye, and a small telescope will be needed in order to differentiate the stars.

## ERIDANUS - THE RIVER

**Mythology:**

The river Eridanus is one of the most famous rivers in Greek mythology. It was the river that the youth Phaethon fell into when he was struck down while foolishly flying Apollo's chariot through the sky (see Cygnus). Appolonius mentions it in "Jason and the Golden Fleece". After Phaethon fell into the river his friend Cygnus dove in after him to retrieve the body of his fallen friend, for which the Gods rewarded him by setting his image in the sky as Cygnus the swan. Rivers have often figured significantly as symbols in Greek Mythology. A well known example is the River Styx, which had to be crossed to get into the underworld.

**Visibility:** November - February

**Location:** This giant constellation is located in both the Southern and Northern Hemispheres. Eridanus is bordered by Orion Taurus, Cetus, Fornax, Phoenix, Horologium, Caelum, and Lepus.

**Special Features:** Eridanus is such an expansive constellation, that it is bound to have several interesting objects. The most impressive star in the constellation is Archenar, a blue white star with an exceptional magnitude of -0.5. For the beginner, however, there is another, more important sight. A white dwarf (see astronomical terms), visible through small telescopes can be seen, as well as a nearby orbiting red dwarf (see astronomical terms).

## FORNAX - THE FURNACE

**Quick Facts:** Fornax was discovered by the French astronomer Nicholas Louis de Lacaille in the 1750's.

**Visibility:** August - November

**Location:** Fornax is a Southern Hemisphere constellation which borders Sculptor, Cetus, and

Eridanus.

**Special Features:** The most interesting sight in Fornax is Fornacis, a binary made up of two yellow stars boasting a modest magnitude of 4.0 and 6.5 respectively.

## GEMINI - THE TWINS

**Mythology:** The constellation of Gemini is based on the legend of Castor and Pollux (also known as the Dioscuri), who were the twin sons of Leda and Zeus. They were the result of a coupling between the two when Zeus disguised himself as a swan, in order to seduce her. It is said that because of this, Leda actually laid an egg rather than giving birth. Whatever the case, Castor and Pollux were great heroes. Both of them were fierce rivals, but inseparable. Each of them was immensely gifted in the skills of battle. Castor was known as a warrior and horseman, while Pollux was an Olympic champion in boxing. The Dioscuri, like most Greek heroes, seemed to have spent their lives doing nothing but travelling the world and fighting anyone who would accept their challenge. They fought bravely with Jason and the Argonauts, but perhaps they are most famous for their battle with their cousins, Idas and Lyceneus. The argument between the two sets of cousins erupted after they were dividing a bull they had just killed. Idas suggested that he would divide the bull into four quarters, and the first two that finished their shares should have the rest. At saying this, Idas bolted for the bull and devoured his portion, and then helped his brother finish his, thus winning the rest of the meat. Castor and Pollux felt cheated, and decided to make war on their rivals land, stealing all of their cattle. This led directly to an all out battle between them. In their struggle, Castor and Lyceneus were killed. Just when Idas was about to kill Pollux, Zeus saved his son and struck down Idas with a lightning bolt. Zeus then tried to take Pollux up to Olympia to become an immortal, but he refused to go without his brother. Zeus then decided to let each of them spend half of their time in Olympia, and half in the underworld.

**Visibility:** November - June

**Location:** Gemini is a Northern Hemisphere constellation bordering Auriga, Taurus, Orion, Monoceros, Canis Minor, Cancer and Lynx.

**Special Features:** Gemini is an excellent constellation for star-gazing, whatever your level of expertise. Historically it has been made famous as the point of the discovery for both Uranus and Pluto. One of the best starting points for any amateur is to identify the "twin stars" of Castor and Pollux, named after the legendary twins of Greek mythology. Pollux is the greater of the two. A yellow giant, with a magnitude of 1.1 it is easily visible to the naked eye. Castor is a blue white star, with a magnitude of 1.6. The best time to take a look at these two stars is on the 14th of December when one of the most productive meteor showers visible occurs near Castor. There is also a meteor shower to watch for on the 19th of October.

## GRUS - THE CRANE

**Quick Facts:** Frederick de Houtman and Pieter Dirkszoon Keyser discovered Grus in the late 16th Century.

**Visibility:** Not visible from Great Britain.

**Location:** Grus is a Southern Hemisphere constellation, bordering Microscopium, Indus, Tucana, Phoenix, Sculptor, and Piscis Austrinus.

**Special Features:** The outline of a crane is easily seen through the configuration of the stars in Grus. Although there are no spectacular objects, there are a series of interesting double stars. The most impressive of the stars in the constellation is Alnair, which makes the axis of an incongruent cross. It is a blue white star with a magnitude of 1.7. The head of the crane is made by the third brightest star in the constellation, known as Al Dhanab, a giant blue white star with a magnitude of 3.0.

## HERCULES

**Mythology:** Hercules, is without doubt, the most famous of the Greek heroes. In fact, he is probably better known today than any of the Greek Gods. His legend has lasted for such a long time, and has been expanded upon so often that it is difficult to summarise his amazing exploits. His most famous deeds are the "twelve labours" which were so celebrated, that their legend has figured prominently in the stories of nine constellations. Hercules' parents (Amphitryon and Alcmene) were both mortals. His real father, however, was Zeus, who came to Alcmene in the guise of her husband, Amphitryon. Zeus' wife Hera, who was never happy with her husbands philandering, took an immediate dislike to Hercules, as he was a living symbol of her husbands infidelity. To add to her anger, Hermes took the baby Hercules to suckle on Hera's breast while she was sleeping, thus, making him even more powerful. When Hera woke up and realised what was happening, she threw Hercules off her, and the milk that spilled from her breast is said to have fallen into the sky and created the Milky Way. When Hercules was still a baby, Hera put two deadly snakes in his crib. Amphitryon came running in to save his son, but his help wasn't necessary, as Hercules, at the age of eight months, had already killed them both.

When Hercules grew older, his cousin Eurystheus challenged him to complete ten labours. These labours, however, were actually conceived by Hera, who was still very bitter towards Hercules. She was constantly trying to make his road as hard as possible, hoping that he would be killed along the way. His first labour was to kill the Nemean Lion (see Leo for details). Second was to kill the Lernaean Hydra (see Hydra for details). This deed was not counted in the ten because Hercules used the help of his nephew, Iolaus. His third labour was to capture alive the Erymanthian Bear, which he managed to do by chasing it to the point of exhaustion. His fourth labour was to capture the Hind of Ceryneia, which was considered an act of sacrilege.

After hunting it for a year, Hercules was able to capture it. He also argued his case so eloquently that he was not punished by the Gods for his impious actions. The fifth labour was to kill the Stymphalian Birds, who were known for their steel wings and claws. Hercules managed to kill them by shooting them with his arrows, which had been dipped in the blood of the Hydra. The sixth labour was the extremely unenviable task of cleaning the massive Stables of Augias. King Augias had never bothered to have his stables cleaned, and as a result of this, the job had become almost impossible. Amazingly, Hercules managed to clean them in one day by diverting two rivers to run through the stables. Eurystheus refused to count the stables as a labour, because Hercules received payments for his efforts. The seventh labour was to capture the Cretan Bull, alive. One legend has it that this was the bull which Zeus turned himself into, in order to abduct Europa, which then became the constellation Taurus. The eighth labour was to bring the flesh eating Horses of Diomedes back to Eurystheus, alive. Hercules accomplished this by feeding Diomedes, himself, to the horses, and thus pacifying their hunger for the journey. The ninth labour was to retrieve The Girdle of Queen Hippolyta, which Hercules managed after fighting the Amazons. The Tenth Labour was to drive The Cattle of Geryon from Libya back to Greece. The Eleventh Labour was to go into the Underworld and take Cerberus, the dog who guards the gates of the Underworld, back to the surface. While retrieving the dreaded Cerberus, he managed to save Theseus, who was being held captive by Hades (The God of the Underworld). His twelfth and final labour was to steal The Golden Apples of the Hesperides. In the process of doing so, he killed the dragon that guarded them. The Dragon was consequently set in the sky as a constellation (see Draco).

**Visibility:** March - November

**Location:** Hercules is a Northern Hemisphere constellation, which borders Draco, Bootes, Corona Borealis, Serpens, Ophiuchus, Aquila, and Lyra.

**Special Features:** Hercules is one of the few constellations whose shape coincides with the myth it was named after. It is a huge constellation (the fifth largest), but does not have any one particular star that stands out for the beginner. The best way to identify it is to find the star Vega, in nearby Lyra. Almost directly across from it is Hercules' knee. The most impressive feature, beyond the actual shape of the constellation, is a globular cluster, consisting of hundreds of thousand of stars. This beautiful sight is best seen with a small telescope or binoculars, and can be found in his right rib cage.

## HOROLOGIUM - THE PENDULUM CLOCK

**Quick Facts:** Nicholas Louis de Lacaille discovered Horologium in the 1750s.

**Visibility:** Not visible from Great Britain.

**Location:** Horologium is a Southern Hemisphere constellation, which borders Eridanus, Hydrus,

Reticulum, Dorado and Caelum.

**Special Features:** Horologium is a peculiar constellation, linking two groups of stars across a vast area of space. The outline is closer to that of a sickle, or a fly fishing rod than a pendulum clock. The most impressive feature in Horologium is Alpha Horologii, a yellow giant with a magnitude of 3.9. It is squeezed between Eridanus and Caelum, and is cut off from the rest of the constellation.

## HYDRA - THE WATER SNAKE

**Mythology:** Hydra was a fearsome, six headed monster, whose breath alone could kill any mortal. Hydra was raised by Hera for the sole purpose of killing Hercules. It was in their famous battle that Hydra gained her fame. The second of Hercules' famous labours was to kill Hydra. He did this with the help of his nephew, Iolaus. Hercules shot arrows at the monster, but it had little affect. He tried to cut one of its many heads but this was a fruitless effort, because the second he did, another would grow back in its place. Hercules instructed Iolaus to burn the stump after he had cut off the heads thus stopping them from growing back. Once he did this Hercules was able to get to the centre head and, eventually, kill Hydra. Zeus put Hydra's image in the sky to commemorate the battle.

**Visibility:** January - June

**Location:** Hydra is a Northern Hemisphere constellation bordering, Cancer, Sextans, Crater,

Corvus, Virgo, Libra, Lupus, Antlia, Pyxis, and Monoceros.

**Special Features:** The one thing that stands out above all in Hydra, is the sheer enormity of it. Hydra is the largest constellation in the sky. It literally "snakes" through so many constellations across the sky, it is very hard to identify the whole thing at once. The most prominent part of the snake is the head, which is made up of five stars in an awkward circle. All of these stars have a magnitude between 3 and 5, and serve as a good starting point in looking at Hydra. Another point of interest is the meteor shower known as Hybrids, which can be seen in Hydra on the 11th of December.

# HYDRUS - THE LESSER WATER SNAKE

**Quick Facts:** Frederick de Houtman and Pieter Dirkszoon Keyser discovered Hydrus in the late 16th Century.

**Visibility:** Not visible from Great Britain.

**Location:** Hydrus is a Southern Hemisphere constellation bordering Eridanus, Phoenix, Tucana, Octans, Mensa, Dorado, Reticulum, and Horologium.

**Special Features:** The lesser water snake contains a few interesting objects for the beginner. It is located in the relatively baron area of the South celestial pole. It can most easily be found by first identifying the star in Eridanus, known as Achernar, and then going directly South.

## INDUS - THE INDIAN

**Quick Facts:** Discovered in the late 16th Century by Frederick de Houtman and Pieter Dirkszoon Keyser, it is meant to represent a Native American (Indian).

**Visibility:** Not visible from Great Britain.

**Location:** Indus is a Southern Hemisphere constellation bordering Microscopium, Sagittarius, Telescopium, Octans, Tucana, and Grus.

**Special Features:** Indus is a faint but neat constellation, close to the South celestial pole. The main point of interest is Alpha Indi, an orange giant with a magnitude of 3.1, and a yellow dwarf located very close to the Sun, with a magnitude of 4.7.


## LACERTA - THE LIZARD

**Quick Facts:** Discovered by the famous Polish astronomer Johannes Hevelius in 1687.

**Visibility:** All year.

**Location:** Lacerta is a Northern Hemisphere constellation, located between its far more famous neighbours Cassiopeia, Andromeda, Pegasus, Cygnus, and Cepheus.

**Special Features:** Lacerta, an otherwise indistinct constellation, has gained some notoriety, because of the discovery of what was thought to be a variable star, although to this day there is still some controversy over what it is. It is thought that this object, known as BL Lac, may be some sort of quasar. However, since it does not have the normal signs of what we know to be a quasar, it is still a mystery.

# LEO - THE LION

**Mythology:** The constellation of Leo is based on the first of Hercules' legendary twelve labours. There was a great lion that lived in a cave in Nemea. The lion was infamous for killing several of the inhabitants of Nemea, as well as having a skin that was impervious to any known weapon. On his way to find the lion, Hercules met an old peasant whose only son had been devoured by the lion. The old man pleaded with Hercules not to go into the cave, for he would surely die. Hercules told him not to worry, and that he would avenge the death of his son and return alive. Hercules went into the lions cave and tried to shoot it with arrows, but they simply bounced off him. In the end, after using every weapon at his disposal, he realised the only way to kill the lion was to strangle him, which after a ferocious battle he did. He then tried to take the lions pelt, but was unable to, until he cut it with the lions own razor sharp claws. Hercules then made a hood and cloak out of the skin, which would act as protection against any weapon throughout all of his many battles. Zeus put the image of the lion in the sky to commemorate Hercules' first labour.

**Visibility:** December - August

**Location:** Leo is a Northern Hemisphere constellation, which borders Ursa Major, Leo Minor, Cancer, Hydra, Sextans, Crater, Virgo and Coma Berenices.

**Special Features:** Leo is an exciting constellation, which contains everything a beginner looks for. First of all, the shape of Leo does, to some extent, mirror that of a lion, making it easier to identify. Almost the entire form of the lion is visible to the naked eye. Regulus, a blue white star with a magnitude of 1.4, is located at the top of the lion's hind leg. Leo is also home to six spiral galaxies, although it will be necessary to use a telescope to see them. Three of them are located next to each other, below the lion's stomach. Two more are next to each other on his front leg, and the sixth is located just below his tail. Finally, and most spectacularly, are the three meteor showers, which can be seen in Leo on the 26th of February, the 17th of April and the 17th of November. The meteor shower in November is special because every 33 years it produces unbelievable showers of tens of thousands of meteors, every hour. The next one will be in 1999, so don't forget, you may never see anything like it again.

## LEO MINOR - THE LITTLE LION

**Quick Facts:** Introduced by the Polish astronomer Johannes Hevelius in 1687.

**Visibility:** December - August

**Location:** Leo Minor is a Northern Hemisphere constellation, bordering Ursa Major, Lynx, Cancer, and Leo.

**Special Features:** Leo Minor is not as spectacular as its larger, and older, brother Leo. It can be found by looking South of Ursa Major, and then finding Leo, which appears quite vividly in the sky. Once you have located these two find the series of fainter stars in between the two constellations. That is Leo Minor. The main star in the constellation is a yellow giant double star with a magnitude of 4.2.

## LEPUS - THE HARE

**Quick Facts:** There is no specific myth about the Hare in Greek mythology but as it is located in the sky at the foot of Orion the hunter, it represents one of the animals that Orion is forever chasing through the sky.

**Location:** Lepus is a Northern hemisphere constellation, bordering Orion, Eridanus, Caelum, Canis Major, and Monoceros.

**Visibility:** December - April

**Special Features:** Lepus is an interesting constellation, made most famous for what is known as Hind's "Crimson Star". This star is named after the British astronomer, JR Hind, who described it as "a drop of blood against a black sky". It can be found on the border of Eridanus. Unfortunately, a small telescope will be required to make it out.

## LIBRA - THE SCALES OF JUSTICE

**Mythology:** The myth behind the constellation Libra is taken from an ancient Syrian legend concerning Adonis. He was born when his mother, who had been turned into a tree, was chopped down. Out sprang the baby Adonis. Aphrodite, the Goddess of Love, was so taken by Adonis, that she decided to take him into her own care. She realised that she would not be able to take care of him all year long, so she summoned her sister, Persephone (see Virgo), from the underworld.

Persephone was equally taken by the beauty of the child, and they decided to share the parenting of Adonis. Persephone would take care of her in the six months that she lived on Earth, and when she returned to the underworld, Aphrodite would care for him. As Adonis grew, however, they both became closer to him, and did not want to part with him for half of the year. They argued incessantly until Zeus ordered them to see Themis, the goddess of Law. Themis decided that they should each have Adonis for four months while the remaining four months would be left to Adonis to decide. Zeus was so impressed with the wisdom of Themis, that he put the scales of justice in the sky to honour her . We know them today as Libra.

**Visibility:** May - August

**Location:** Libra is a Northern Hemisphere constellation bordering Serpens, Virgo, Centaurus, Lupus, Scorpius, and Ophiuchus.

**Special Features:** Although Libra is not an extremely bright constellation it can be seen with the naked eye fairly easily, and looks remarkably like the scales of justice, for which it is named. The most interesting feature in Libra is that it is home to Zubeneschamali, one of the only known green stars. It is the second brightest star in the constellation, and can be located on the left side of the triangle that holds the scales.

## LUPUS - THE WOLF

**Quick Facts:** Although Lupus has been recognised since Greek times, it is one of those rare constellations that has no definite myth attached to it. The Greeks simply thought of it as a wild beast killed, by a centaur (neighbouring Centaurus).

**Visibility:** June - August

**Location:** Lupus is a Northern Hemisphere constellation, bordering Centaurus, Circinus, Norma, Scorpius, and Libra.

**Special Features:** The two main stars in Lupus are located close to each other, on the east side of the constellation, near Centaurus. The first is a blue giant, with a magnitude of 2.3 and the second is a giant blue-white star, with a magnitude of 2.7. One of the most interesting objects in Lupus is the open cluster of well over a hundred stars. This can be found just North of the point where Lepus, Circinus and Norma meet.

## LYNX - THE LYNX

**Quick Facts:** The Polish astronomer Johannes Hevelius discovered this constellation in 1687. Named for the spotted wild cat, which was considered a god in Egyptian Mythology.

**Visibility:** All year.

**Location:** Lynx is a Northern Hemisphere constellation, bordering Camelopardalis, Auriga, Gemini, Cancer, Leo Minor, and Ursa Major.

**Special Features:** Lynx is a faint constellation, but it can best be found by first finding Ursa Major, and then finding Castor and Pollux in Gemini, between these two constellations is Lynx. The most prominent feature in Lynx is a red giant, with a magnitude of 3.2. It is located just North of the border of Leo and Leo Minor.

## LYRA - THE LYRE

**Mythology:** The constellation Lyra symbolises the legend of Orpheus and his lyre. Orpheus was renowned throughout heaven and Earth as the greatest of all musicians. In fact, the music that he created with his lyre was able to charm any living being. This was indeed a fortuitous talent at times for Orpheus. When he sailed with Jason and the Argonauts, he saved the crew from being seduced by the enchanting voices of the Sirens, by playing even more beautifully than they could sing. Orpheus is most famous for his ill-fated attempt to save his wife, Euridice, from the Underworld. Orpheus was so saddened by his wife's death that he refused to accept it. He followed her down to the Underworld, and was able to charm everyone there, including Hades and Persephone, who decided in the end to give Euridice a second life on Earth, but on the condition that Orpheus would not look back at her until they had reached the Earth's surface. Just before Orpheus was about to step back onto the surface, he could not stop himself from checking if his wife was still behind him. Of course, the second he did, his wife was returned forever to the Underworld, and Hades refused Orpheus a second chance. Upon his death, Orpheus' lyre was set in the sky, forever commemorating his talent.

**Visibility:** All year.

**Location:** Lyra is a Northern Hemisphere

constellation, bordering Cygnus Vulpecula, Hercules, and Draco.

**Special Features:** Lyra is home to one of the brightest, and well known, stars in the sky, Vega, which makes up part of the Summer Triangle (see Locating a Star). Vega, a blue-white star, with a magnitude of 0.3, will, in a mere 12,000 years, take over for Polaris as the "North Star". Another fascinating sight in Lyra is the planetary nebula, located between the constellation's other two most prominent stars, Sulafat and Sheliak.

## MENSA - THE TABLE MOUNTAIN

**Quick Facts:** This faint constellation was first recorded by the French astronomer Nicholas Louis de Lacaille. Mensa was named in honour of Table Mountain on the Cape of Good Hope.

**Visibility:** Not visible from Great Britain.

**Location:** Mensa is a Southern Hemisphere constellation, which borders Octans, Hydrus, Dorado, Volans, and Chameleon.

**Special Features:** The most interesting feature in Mensa is the huge Magellanic cloud that creeps over from its Northern neighbour, Dorado.

## MICROSCOPIUM - THE MICROSCOPE

**Quick Facts:** This constellation was first recorded by the French astronomer Nicholas Louis de Lacaille in the 1750's.

**Visibility:** August - October

**Location:** Microscopium is a Southern Hemisphere

constellation, bordering Capricornus, Sagittarius, Telescopium, Indus, Grus, and Piscis Austrinus.

**Special Features:** Microscopium is a faint constellation, featuring two giant yellow stars, with magnitudes just under five. There is also a blue white star, with a magnitude of 4.7.

## MONOCEROS - THE UNICORN

**Quick Facts:** This rather intriguing constellation was first recorded by the Dutch astronomer Petrus Plancius in 1613. It was named in honour of the mythological horse with a horn protruding from its forehead.

**Visibility:** December - April

**Location:** Monoceros is a Northern Hemisphere constellation, bordering Orion Lepus, Canis Minor, Puppis, Hydra, Gemini and Taurus.

**Special Features:** Monoceros is packed with interesting features. Most notably is the Rosette Nebula, which encompasses a star cluster. Although the Nebula is faint, the star cluster can be seen with a pair of binoculars or small telescope. Monoceros is also home to "Placket's Star", which is the largest known double star. Unfortunately, the stars are located so far away that they have a magnitude of 6.1, and cannot be seen without the aid of binoculars or a small telescope.

## MUSCA - THE FLY

**Quick Facts:** Discovered by the Dutch astronomers Frederick de Houtman and Pieter Dirkszoon Keyser in the late 16th Century.

**Visibility:** Not visible from Great Britain.

**Location:** Musca is a Southern Hemisphere constellation, bordering Crux, Caring, Chameleon, Circinus, and Centaurus.

**Special Features:** The brightest star in Musca is Alpha Muscae, a blue white star with a magnitude of 2.7. The most interesting feature however, is a large globular cluster of stars that can be seen with a pair of binoculars or a small telescope. This cluster is located South of Alpha Muscae, along the outline of the fly.

## NORMA - THE LEVEL

**Quick Facts:** This minor constellation was introduced by the French astronomer Nicholas Louis de Lacaille in the 1750's.

**Visibility:** Not visible from Great Britain.

**Location:** Norma is a Southern Hemisphere constellation, which borders Lupus, Circinus, Triangulum Australe, Ara, and Scorpius.

**Special Features:** Norma is a tiny and precise constellation, whose five stars form a right angle. The most interesting features in the constellation are its three open clusters and its planetary nebula.

## OCTANS - THE OCTANT

**Quick Facts:** Octans was discovered in the 1750's by the French Astronomer Nicholas Louis de Lacaille

**Visibility:** Not visible from Great Britain

**Location:** Octans is located at the South Pole, and is

bordered by Chameleon, Mensa, Hydrus, Tucana, Pavo, Apus, and Musca.

**Special Features:** A quick glance at a map of the night sky will tell you immediately what the most interesting feature is in the constellation. It contains the South celestial pole and Alpha Octanis, a white and yellow binary star that serves as the South Star. Unfortunately, Alpha Octanis only has a magnitude of 5.2, and thus is not as useful or as famous as Polaris, the North Star.

## OPHIUCHUS - THE SERPENT HOLDER

**Mythology:** The Serpent Holder is a rather misleading name for Ophiuchus, which comes from the myth of the first and greatest doctor, Aesculapius. He was renowned throughout the world for his medical prowess, including being the ship's doctor with Jason and the Argonauts. He gained his place in the sky, however, for unlocking the secrets to eternal life. It is said that one day Aescupalis had killed a snake, and then to his amazement watched as another snake came over and administered a herb to his fallen friend. The snake came back to life, and Aescupalis immediately took the herb from the snake and began experimenting on its use for human patients. Aescupalis became so skilled with the herb, that he began to be able to save the lives of some of Greece's fallen heroes. This news was not well received by Hades, who as God of the underworld, would lose power if the steady stream of mortal deaths did not file into his dark lair. Hades complained to Zeus, who agreed with Hades that it was man's lot to be mortal, and struck Aescupalis down with a lightning bolt. Zeus realised, however, that Aescupalis' accomplishments should be recognised, and set him in the sky as the constellation Ophiuchus.

**Visibility:** April - July

**Location:** Ophiuchus is located in the Northern and Southern Hemispheres and is bordered by Hercules, Serpens, Scorpius, and Sagittarius.

**Special Features:** Ophiuchus is a large constellation, the eleventh largest in the sky. It is best known for being the home to "Barnard's Star", named after its discoverer, the American astronomer EE Barnard. This star, a red dwarf (see astronomical terms) gained its notoriety for being second closest star to the Earth. Despite its proximity to the Earth, it still only has a magnitude of 9.5 because of its size. This is extremely fortunate for us on Earth, as the possibility of having two stars with the power of the Sun would have made it impossible for most forms of life to have developed. The other interesting feature of "Barnard's Star" is that astronomers suspect that it may have planets of its own, because of its peculiar rotation. Ophiuchus is also home to meteor showers on the 13th of June.

# ORION - THE HUNTER

**Mythology:** The legend of Orion is one of the more celebrated in Greek mythology. Orion was not only a giant, and according to some stories able to walk on water, but he was considered the greatest hunter to have ever lived. Although there are several myths which often contradict each other, he is probably best known for his feats on the island of Hyria. Orion fell in love with Merope, who was the granddaughter of the God Dionysus. Her father, Oenopion, had promised her hand to Orion if he put his formidable hunting skills to work, and freed the island of the many beasts which threatened the Hyrian population. Orion began his task immediately, and would return every night with the pelts of the beasts, until he had killed them all. He then demanded to marry Merope, but her father claimed, falsely, that there were still wild animals deep in the woods. Orion, knowing this to be a lie, planned to elope with Merope. To prevent Orion from doing this, Oenopion blinded him when he was sleeping. Sightless, Orion travelled to the end of the world, with the help of a child, whom he carried on his shoulders to guide him. Finally, when he reached the horizon, he looked directly into the Sun, where Helios (The Sun God) returned his sight. Along his travels, Orion forgot about Merope, and fell in love with Aurora. It was, however, a short-lived relationship as Orion was killed by a giant scorpion (for details see Scorpius).

**Visibility:** November - April

**Location:** Orion is a Northern hemisphere constellation, which borders Taurus, Eridanus, Lepus, Monoceros, and Gemini.

**Special Features:** Orion has absolutely everything one could want in a constellation. Its form as a hunter, with his shield in one hand, his club in another and his sword hanging from his belt, is so life-like that it is easy to see how ancient civilisations thought that this was truly a man set in the sky. One of the most amazing features in Orion is his belt, made up of three very bright stars, perfectly spaced, creating his waist line. Hanging from the celestial belt is his green sword, which is actually the Orion Nebula. The Orion Nebula is without doubt the most famous nebula in the sky. It is visible to the naked eye, and is packed with a host of bright double stars, which are also distinctly visible. The two most prominent stars in the constellation are Betelgeuse and Rigel. Betelgeuse, Orion's right shoulder, is a red super-giant with a fluctuating magnitude of 1.3 to 0.4. Rigel, the hunter's left foot, is a blue super-giant, with a magnitude of 0 and an absolute magnitude of -7.1. Orion also has meteor showers on the 21st of October and the 10th and 11th of December.

## Pavo - The Peacock

**Quick Facts:** Pavo was discovered by Frederick de Houtman and Pieter Dirkszoon Keyser in the late 16th Century.

**Visibility:** Not visible from Great Britain.

**Location:** Pavo is a Southern Hemisphere constellation, close to the South Pole. It borders Telescopium, Ara, Triangulum Australe, Octans, and Indus.

**Special Features:** Easily the most prominent star in

Pavo is Pavonis, which symbolise the Peacock's eye in the constellation, and is located at the corner of Telescopium and Indus. Pavonis is a blue white star, with a magnitude of 1.9. There is also a significant globular cluster in the Northern section of the constellation, which is visible through binoculars.

## PEGASUS - THE WINGED HORSE

**Mythology:** Pegasus, the beautiful white winged stallion, was created from a very unlikely source, the blood of Medusa. Medusa was a beautiful maiden, whom Poseidon had fallen in love with. She was especially noted for her flowing, golden hair. Unfortunately for Medusa, she made a mistake common to beautiful Greek maidens. She compared herself with Hera. Such a claim usually led to Hera's immediate revenge. In Medusa's case, her hair was turned to snakes, and her face made so hideous that anyone who looked at her would turn instantly to stone. Perseus was sent to cut off her head, and while carrying it back to Greece, drops of her blood fell into the sea. Poseidon, seeing this, and remembering the love he once had for her, mixed the blood with the sea. In doing so he created the virgin birth of Pegasus, the one and only winged horse. Other versions of this story claim that Pegasus sprang out of Medusa's head upon decapitation. Whatever the case, Pegasus would go on to play a rather minor role in Greek mythology. Despite this, Pegasus, and the magical idea of a winged horse, has managed to stay in the minds of people all over the world to the present day, while other, far more important characters, have slipped out of popular memory.

**Visibility:** July - February

**Location:** Pegasus is a Northern Hemisphere constellation bordering Lacerta, Vulpecula, Delphinus, Equuleus, Aquarius, Pisces, and Andromeda.

**Special Features:** The most notable features in this constellation are the four stars which make up the "Square of Pegasus". The most impressive star in the group is Scheat, which is a blue-white giant variable star that has a magnitude of 2.8. Pegasus also has two meteor showers, visible on the 9th of July and on the 12th of November.

## PERSEUS - THE HERO

**Mythology:** Perseus is second only to his ancestor, Hercules, as the greatest hero in Greek mythology . His adventures have figured prominently in the stories of six constellations. One of his most impressive feats was killing the Gorgon Medusa. When Perseus was still a young man, he rashly promised King Polydectes Medusa's head as a tribute. Polydectes held him to his promise, and warned that if Perseus did not provide her head for him, he would take Perseus' mother for his wife. Luckily for Perseus, he was favoured by the Gods. They provided him with winged sandals, which allowed him to fly, a magical helmet which rendered the wearer invisible, and a shield, that was so polished it worked as a mirror. With these tools, Perseus wearily approached Medusa, a creature so horrific that anyone who looked at her would turn to stone. Perseus flew above her and, looking at Medusa's reflection through his shield, decapitated her with his sword. When he returned to pay tribute to Polydectes, he learned that he had tried to abduct his mother, while he was not there to protect her. As punishment for his encroachment, Perseus used Medusa's head to turn Polydectes into stone. He eventually fell in love with, and married, the beautiful princess Andromeda, who is located in the sky next to him. For more on the story of Perseus see Andromeda, Cassiopeia, Pegasus, Cepheus and Cetus.

**Visibility:** All year.

**Location:** Perseus is a Northern Hemisphere constellation, bordering Camelopardalis, Cassiopeia, Triangulum, Aries, Taurus, and Auriga.

**Special Features:** Perseus is an excellent, constellation brimming with celestial objects. The brightest star in the constellation is Algenib. Located in the centre of Perseus Algenib is a yellow super-giant ,with a magnitude of 1.8, and is visible to the naked eye. Perseus is also home to the "California Nebula", and no less than eight star clusters. Although some of these clusters are quite spectacular, the easiest one to find with just a pair of binoculars is located on the border of Andromeda, and is home to about sixty stars.

## PHOENIX - THE PHOENIX

**Quick Facts:** Phoenix was first recorded by the Dutch

navigators Frederick de Houtman and Pieter Dirkszoon Keyser in the late 16th Century. The constellation was named in honour of the legendary Egyptian bird, who would erupt into flames and then rise again out of its own ashes every five hundred years.

**Visibility:** Not visible from Great Britain.

**Location:** Phoenix is a Southern Hemisphere constellation, bordering Sculptor, Grus, Tucana, Hydrus, Eridanus, and Fornax.

**Special Features:** Phoenix is one of those constellations that does appear to mirror the form it is named after. The brightest star in the constellation is Phoenicis, a yellow giant with a magnitude of 2.4. It is home to two meteor showers, one on the 14th of July and another on the 5th of December.

## PICTOR - THE PAINTER'S EASEL

**Quick Facts:** This Southern Hemisphere constellation was discovered by the French astronomer Nicholas Louis de Lacaille in the 1750s.

**Visibility:** Not visible from Great Britain.

**Location:** Pictor is a Southern Hemisphere constellation, bordering Columba, Caelum, Dorado, Volans, Carina, and Puppis.

**Special Features:** Pictor is a small constellation best known for its location near the famous star Canopus, in neighbouring Carina. The brightest star in the constellation is Pictoris, a white star with a magnitude of 3.3.

## PISCES - THE FISH

**Mythology:** The Greek myth surrounding the Zodiac sign Pisces, is based on the story of Aphrodite (the Goddess of Love), her son Eros (better known to us today as Cupid), and Poseidon's giant fish, who came to their rescue. Eros was playing in the woods when he came upon Typhon, who was the most horrible of all monsters in Greek mythology Typhon was created with only one purpose in mind, to kill the Gods. His body took the form of several snakes, his fingers were dragon heads, and his eyes shot forth flames. All of the Gods, except for Zeus, were powerless against him. Eros ran to his mother and then, panic stricken, they fled for their lives. In their haste to escape, they took a wrong turn, and ended up with Typhon behind them and only the sea in front of them. They were trapped and helpless. Aphrodite and Eros stood there, awaiting their fate when two fish rose from the sea, followed by Poseidon, God of the Sea. Poseidon told them to climb on to the fish, and they carried them out to sea and safety. Poseidon then put the image of the two fish in the sky, to commemorate their good deed.

**Visibility:** September - December

**Location:** Pisces is a Northern Hemisphere constellation, bordering Triangulum, Andromeda, Pegasus, Aquarius, Cetus, and Aries.

**Special Features:** Pisces is a sprawling constellation (the fourteenth largest in the sky), and is best known for being home to the vernal equinox. The vernal equinox occurs when the Sun passes from the

Southern into the Northern celestial hemisphere, marking the beginning of Spring. This point will move into Aquarius in several hundred years, thus starting the famous "Age of Aquarius". The brightest star in the constellation is Alrescha, a blue-white double star with a combined magnitude of 3.8. There are two meteor showers in Pisces, one occurring on the 20th of September, and the other on the 12th of October.

## PISCIS AUSTRINUS - THE SOUTHERN FISH

**Quick Facts:** Pisces Austrinus is another of the rare constellations known in Greek times, with no specific myth attached to it. It is often pictured drinking the water from Gannymedes (Aquarius) urn.

**Visibility:** September - November

**Location:** Piscis Austrinus is a Southern Hemisphere constellation, bordering Aquarius, Capricornus, Microscopium, Grus, Sculptor, and Cetus.

**Special Features:** The greatest point of interest in Pisces Austrinus is Formalhaut, an interesting, blue-white star with a magnitude of 1.2., located near the border of Sculptor. Pisces Austrinus also has a collection of interesting double stars. A pair of binoculars is required to differentiate them.

## PUPPIS - THE STERN

**Quick Facts:** Puppis was once a part of Argo Navis the ship sailed by Jason and the Argonauts. Puppis (the stern of the ship) was separated by the French astronomer Nicholas Louis de Lacaille in 1763.

**Visibility:** January - April

**Location:** Puppis is a Northern Hemisphere constellation, located in the Milky Way, and is bordered by Monoceros, Canis Major, Columba, Pictor, Carina, Veal, Pyxis and Hydra.

**Special Features:** Puppis, lying as it does in the Milky Way, is a fertile hunting ground for stars. The brightest star in the constellation is a blue-white super-giant, located near the border of Vela and Pyxis, with a magnitude of 2.2.

## PYXIS - THE COMPASS

**Quick Facts:** This modest constellation was first outlined by the French astronomer Nicholas Louis de Lacaille in the 1750s. It was named in honour of the compass used by astronomers to help chart the sky.

**Visibility:** February - May

**Location:** Pyxis is a Southern Hemisphere constellation which lies in the Milky Way. It is bordered by Hydra, Puppis, Veal, Antlia, and Hydra.

**Special Features:** Pyxis is a small constellation , and although it is located in the Milky Way, it does not have a great deal of easily visible objects. The brightest star in the constellation, Pyxidis is a blue-white giant star with a magnitude of 3.7. The most significant object is a variable star known as T Pyx, whose magnitude is capable of changing from 14 to 6. This occurrence, however, is rather erratic, and happens approximately every 21 years.

## RETICULUM - THE NET

**Quick Facts:** This tiny but attractive constellation, was discovered by Nicholas Louis de Lacaille in the 1750's.

**Visibility:** Not visible from Great Britain

**Location:** Reticulum is located near the South Pole, and it is encompassed by Horologium, Hydrus, and Dorado.

**Special Features:** One of the smallest constellations is formed by six stars making a neat and precise diamond. The brightest star in the constellation is a yellow giant star, with a magnitude of 3.4.

## SAGITTA - THE ARROW

**Quick Facts:** This miniature constellation is another that dates back to Greek times, but has no corresponding mythology, except that it is seen as an arrow shot from the neighbouring constellation of Hercules.

**Visibility:** July - November

**Location:** Sagitta is a Northern Hemisphere constellation, bordered by Vulpecula, Hercules, Aquila, and Delphinus.

**Special Features:** Sagitta is a tiny constellation, the third smallest in the sky. Despite its size, it manages to illustrate the image of an arrow flying through the sky quite convincingly. The brightest object in the constellation is a yellow giant with a magnitude of 4.4. The most interesting feature in Sagitta is a star cluster, located towards the head of the arrow. It can be seen with the aid of binoculars or a small telescope.

## SAGITTARIUS - THE ARCHER

**Mythology:** With the exception of Pholus and Chiron (see Centaurus), Centaurs were generally regarded as vicious creatures. Their bodies were composed of the four legs and torso of a horse and the head and arms of a human. Their weapon was a bow and arrow, which is why the constellation is known as "The Archer". The Centaurs were involved in several dubious adventures, the most famous of which involved the hero Hercules. Legend has it that Hercules had gone to visit Pholus, one of the two Centaurs who were not hostile to humans. After eating in his cave, Hercules convinced Pholus to open a bottle of wine, that was only to be drunk when all of the centaurs were present. As soon as they began to drink, the sweet bouquet of the wine wafted through the air and caught the attention of the other centaurs. Enraged by the thought that they were not sharing in the wine, the Centaurs galloped towards the unsuspecting duo and attacked with every weapon available. Hercules was able to fight them off with his poison arrows, and fought with such fury that he was able to force the normally fierce Centaurs off . They ran to the cave in which Chiron lived, and surrounded him. Hercules continued shooting his arrows at the Centaurs, and accidentally struck down the kindly Chiron.

**Visibility:** July - September

**Location:** Sagittarius is a Northern and Southern

Hemisphere constellation, bordering Aquila, Scutum, Ophiuchus, Scorpius, Corona Australis, Telescopium, Indus, Microscopium, and Capricornus.

**Special Features:** Sagittarius is a fantastic constellation, replete with every possible celestial object. In fact there is no constellation that has more objects to look at. Among the many stars that make up Sagittarius, there are eight that create what is known as the "teapot". The brightest star in the constellation, it also makes up part of the interior constellation of the "teapot". Kaus Australis is a blue-white giant with a magnitude of 1.8. There are three nebulas in the constellation. The easiest one for the novice to identify is known as the "Lagoon Nebula", which is visible to the naked eye, but is better when seen through binoculars, or a small telescope.

## SCORPIUS - THE SCORPION

**Mythology:** The mythology behind Scorpius is based on the story of the battle between the two great hunters in Greek mythology, Orion and Artemis. There are several different versions of the legend. However, all of them have the same basic story-line, which involves Artemis summoning up a scorpion to kill Orion for his indiscretions. In one legend, Orion challenges Artemis to a hunting competition, in which he angers Artemis by needlessly slaughtering animals just for his honour. In another version, Orion attacks Artemis herself. In still another, he angers Artemis by trying to seduce one of her servants. Unfortunately for Orion, they all end with him being killed by a giant scorpion. The scorpion was set in the sky as the constellation Scorpius, and can be seen forever chasing the constellation Orion around the sky.

**Visibility:** June - August

**Location:** Scorpius is ideally located in a rich section of the Milky Way, and is in both the Northern and Southern Hemispheres. Scorpius borders Ophiuchus, Libra, Lupus, Norma, Ara, Corona Australis, and Sagittarius.

**Special Features:** Scorpius is an excellent constellation for the amateur astronomer, as it is filled with interesting objects. The striking thing about Scorpius is that it mirrors the image of a stinging scorpion fairly accurately. The most brilliant point for naked eye observers is Antares, a red variable, double, super giant with an approximate magnitude of 1.0. Antares is not alone, however, as Scorpius is home to several stars that are easily seen with the naked eye. There are also several globular and open clusters in the constellation. The best one for beginners to find is a third magnitude open cluster, consisting of approximately eighty stars. This cluster is located near the border of Sagittarius and Coma Australis. Scorpius also has two meteor showers, visible on the 3rd of May and the 5th of June.

## SCULPTOR - THE SCULPTOR

**Quick Facts:** Sculptor was discovered by the French astronomer Nicholas Louis de Lacaille in the 1750's.

**Visibility:** September - November

**Location:** Sculptor is a Southern Hemisphere constellation, bordering Cetus, Aquarius, Piscis Austrinus, Grus, Phoenix, and Fornax.

**Special Features:** Sculptor is a faint constellation whose brightest object, Sculptoris, is a blue-white giant with a magnitude of 4.3. It is also home to three spiral galaxies and globular cluster, located North-east of Sculptoris.

## SCUTUM - THE SHIELD

**Quick Facts:** Scutum was originally called Scutum Sobiescianum (Sobieski's Shield), in honour of the Polish King, John Sobieski III. It was discovered by the Polish astronomer Johannes Hevelius in 1684

**Visibility:** May - November

**Location:** Scutum is a Northern Hemisphere constellation, bordering Serpens, Sagittarius, and Aquila.

**Special Features:** Scutum is a tiny constellation, whose brightest object is a giant star with a magnitude of 3.9. The most interesting object in the constellation, however, is the incredible star cluster known as the "Wild Duck Cluster". Unfortunately, it is necessary to use a telescope to really appreciate its beauty.

## SERPENS - THE SERPENT

**Mythology:** Serpens is an ancient constellation and, although it does not have its own specific mythology, it is inextricably linked with neighbouring Ophiuchus.

Serpens is meant to represent the snake, which showed Ophiuchus how to give man eternal life. For more on this story see Ophiuchus.

**Visibility:** March - October

**Location:** Serpens is a Northern Hemisphere constellation that is divided into two sections on either side of Ophiuchus. It borders Bootes, Virgo, Libra, Ophiuchus, Hercules, Scutum, and Aquila.

**Special Features:** Serpens is unique, in that it is the only constellation that is split into two halves. This is because the image of the serpent is wrapped around Ophiuchus (See Ophiuchus background). In the section containing the head of the serpent, lies one of the most amazing, globular clusters in the sky. The 6th magnitude cluster which lies close to the border of Virgo, is easily visible through binoculars or a small telescope.

## SEXTANS - THE SEXTANT

**Quick Facts:** Sextans was discovered by the Polish astronomer Johannes Hevelius in 1687.

**Visibility:** January - June

**Location:** Sextans is a Southern Hemisphere constellation, bordering Leo, hydra, and Crater.

**Special Features:** Sextans is a medium sized constellation, which is most easily found by first drawing a line from Ursa Major on to Leo (Locating a star section), and then extending it on to Sextans. The brightest star in the constellation is Sextanis, a blue-white giant with a magnitude of 4.5.

# TAURUS - THE BULL

**Mythology:** Once again, Zeus is at the heart of a myth. It was tried and true practice for Zeus to assume the form of different animals, in order to gain the trust of an unsuspecting maiden. This time, Europa was the subject of his desire. Zeus had seen her playing on the beach and, as was his wont, he had instantly fallen madly in love with her. Zeus knew that he could not approach her directly, as word of his reputation preceded him. (Not to mention Europa's father, King Agenor, who would not be pleased with Zeus' trying to seduce his daughter). Zeus disguised himself as a perfect, white bull. When Europa saw the bull she was amazed, not only by its colouring, but by its friendly nature. As Europa approached the bull, it kneeled down and beckoned her to climb on. The second she did, Zeus rose to his feet and jumped into the Ocean, swimming all the way to Crete. There, Zeus managed to seduce her, and she bore him three sons. This did not sit well with King Agenor, who ordered his sons to pursue Zeus and retrieve their sister. After many years, Europa's brothers gave up their impossible quest. Zeus was impressed by their attempt, however, and decided to place the image of the bull in the sky, to commemorate the efforts of Europa's brothers.

**Visibility:** October - May

**Location:** Taurus is located in both the Northern and Southern Hemispheres, and is bordered by Auriga, Perseus, Aries, Eridanus, Orion, and Gemini.

**Special Features:** Taurus is absolutely packed with

beautiful objects. The single, brightest object in Taurus is the famous red giant star, known as Aldebaran. Aldebaran has an incredible magnitude of 0.75, and represents the blazing red eye of the bull. The best known feature in Taurus are the Pleiades, better known as the Seven Sisters. They make up the most famous, and striking star cluster in the sky. There are also three meteor showers that can be seen in Taurus, on the 29th of June, and the 3rd and 13th of November.

## TELESCOPIUM - THE TELESCOPE

**Quick Facts:** Telescopium was discovered by the French astronomer Nicholas Louis de Lacaille in the 1750s.

**Visibility:** Not visible from Great Britain.

**Location:** Telescopium is a Southern Hemisphere constellation, and is bordered by Corona Australis, Ara, Pavo, Indus, Microscopium and Sagittarius.

**Special Features:** The outline of Telescopium is quite small, consisting of only four stars making a right angle. Despite this, the area of the constellation is several times larger, giving it a wide area of open space. The brightest object in the constellation is a blue-white star, with a magnitude of 3.5.

## TRIANGULUM - THE TRIANGLE

**Quick Facts:** Triangulum is one of those rare constellations known to the Greeks, but without corresponding mythology. The Greek philosopher and mathematician, Pythagorus, whose famous Pythagorean Theorem dealt with the triangle, could have some bearing on its inclusion amongst the constellations.

**Visibility:** August - March

**Location:** Triangulum is a Northern Hemisphere constellation bordered by Andromeda, Pisces, Aries, and Perseus.

**Special Features:** As one might expect, Triangulum is in the shape of a triangle. It is formed by six stars, the brightest of which is Beta Triangulum, a white giant star with a magnitude of 3.0. Surprisingly, the brightest star in the constellation is not the alpha star which has a magnitude of 3.4. Telescopium is also home to a spiral galaxy, that can be seen with binoculars or a small telescope.

## TRIANGULUM AUSTRALE - THE SOUTHERN TRIANGLE

**Quick Facts:** This Southern constellation was first recorded by the Italian explorer Amerigo Vespucci who is perhaps better known as the person whom the Americas was named for.

**Visibility:** Not visible from Great Britain.

**Location:** Triangulum is neighboured by Norma, Circinus, Apus, and Ara.

**Special Features:** The shape of Triangulum Australe is formed by four stars that create quite an even, though not geometrically perfect, triangle (obviously two of these stars are on the same line). The brightest object in the constellation is an orange giant star with a magnitude of 1.9. Triangulum Australe also shares a star cluster with neighbouring Norma.

## TUCANA -THE TOUCAN

**Quick Facts:** Tucana was discovered by the Dutch astronomers Frederick de Houtman and Pieter Dirkszoon Keyser in the late 16th Century. It is named after the exotic bird found in the Southern Hemisphere.

**Visibility:** Not visible in Great Britain.

**Location:** Tucana is located near the South celestial pole, next to Phoenix, Grus, Indus, Octans and Hydra.

**Special Features:** The brightest object in the constellation is an orange giant, with a magnitude of 2.9. The most interesting feature in Tucana is a gigantic, 4th magnitude Magellanic cloud, located in the Southern section of the constellation.

## URSA MAJOR - THE GREAT BEAR

**Mythology:** The constellation Ursa Major is based in the myth of the nymph Callisto. She spent her days frolicking in the woods with her friend and lover Artemis. One day, Zeus saw her alone in the woods, and fell in love with her. Zeus disguised himself as Artemis and seduced Callisto. She became pregnant, and had a son named Arcas (see Bootes). When Artemis found out about this, she became terribly jealous, and because she was unable to do anything to

Zeus, she turned Callisto into a bear. Years later, Callisto' s son Arcas, who was a great hunter, came upon his mother in the forest, but did not realise who she was. He chased her for miles until she sought cover in a forbidden temple. The penalty for such a trespass was death. When Zeus saw that his former lover was to be killed, he saved her by setting her image in the sky as the constellation Ursa Major.

**Visibility:** All year.

**Location:** Ursa Major is a Northern circumpolar constellation, which borders Draco, Camelopardalis, Lynx, Leo Minor, Canes Venatici, and Bootes.

**Special Features:** Ursa Major also known as the "Plough", or "The Big Dipper" in North America, and is by far the most famous constellation, as well as being the third largest in the sky. If you are just starting out in astronomy, this is the constellation you should begin with. It is always visible in the Northern hemisphere, and is very easy to find. It is also an excellent springboard to find other constellations. For instance, look to the end of the dipper and find Dubhe, a yellow giant, with a magnitude of 1.8. Once you see this star, make a straight line up from it and you will find Polaris, or the "North Star". By doing this, you have not only discovered a new constellation (Ursa Minor), but you can always find North without the use of a compass or map. Another tip is to find the last star in the handle, Alkaid, a blue-white star, with a magnitude of 1.8. This points directly to Arcturus in nearby Bootes. Once you have found Arcturus, it will just take you a few minutes to figure out the rest of Bootes.

## URSA MINOR - THE LITTLE BEAR

**Mythology:** Despite the fact that Ursa Minor is one of the most famous constellations in the sky, there is no particular Greek myth that can be attributed to it. It is thought that the little bear simply represents the companion of Ursa Major, the great bear. The Native American, Hopi Indians, believed the constellation to represent an injured brave being carried on a stretcher. Whilst being followed by his wife, a companion, and a medicine man. There is a somewhat similar Arab legend, which sees the figure as a coffin.

**Visibility:** All year.

**Location:** Ursa Minor encompasses the Northern celestial pole, and is surrounded by Cepheus, Camelopardalis, and Draco.

**Special Features:** There is no doubt as to what is the most interesting feature in Ursa Minor. Polaris, "The North Star", is easily the best known star in the sky, although surprisingly, it is not even close to being the brightest star in the sky. Rather, it is a variable yellow super-giant, with a magnitude of 2.0, which lies almost directly on the North Celestial Pole. Because of precession (see astronomical terms), Polaris is actually moving closer to the exact North Celestial Pole, and will be there, approximately, in the year 2012. Then it will begin moving away from the pole, and will eventually be replaced.

## VELA - THE SAILS

**Quick Facts:** Once a part of the constellation Argo Navis, it was separated into Vela by Nicholas Louis de Lacaille in 1763.

**Visibility:** Not visible from Great Britain

**Location:** Vela is a Southern hemisphere constellation, located in a rich part of the Milky Way, surrounded by Antlia, Pyxis, Puppis, Carina, and Centaurus.

**Special Features:** Lying in the Milky Way, Vela has a number of interesting objects for the amateur astronomer. The brightest point in the constellation is Gamma Velorum, a multiple star made up of two blue-white stars. Vela is perhaps best known for the "Vela Pulsar", but unfortunately this cannot be seen without advanced telescopes. A more easily visible sight is a star cluster located just South of Gamma Velour.

## VIRGO - THE MAIDEN

**Mythology:** The Constellation of Virgo is based on the myths of Demeter, the Goddess of the Harvest, and her daughter Persephone. One day, while Persephone was out picking flowers in a field, the Earth opened in front of her and Hades, the God of the Underworld, appeared. He had fallen in love with the young maiden, and so stole her to become his wife in the underworld. Demeter, who was formerly a very light-hearted soul, went mad with anger over her daughters abduction. She demanded that Persephone be returned to her.

Unfortunately, it was too late, as Persephone, although having abstained from eating or drinking in the underworld for three weeks, had finally given in to her hunger and eaten six pomegranate seeds. Once someone had eaten in the underworld, they could not return to Earth. Demeter could not accept her daughters fate, and as punishment to the world, she disguised herself as a beggar and went to live in a barren frozen wasteland. When she did this, all of the crops on Earth died. The people of Earth began to starve, and there was a great famine. Demeter was unmoved by their cries of hunger. In the end, Zeus was forced to intervene on Demeter' s behalf, and convinced Hades to allow Persephone to spend six months of the year on Earth and six months in the Underworld, for the six seeds she had eaten. Demeter agreed to allow the crops to grow again, but only for the six months that Persephone was with her. It is for this reason that we have approximately six months of warm weather, and six of cold. Zeus put Persephone' s image in the sky as Virgo the Maiden.

**Visibility:** April - July

**Location:** Virgo is neighboured by Bootes, Coma Berenices, Leo, Crater, Corvus, Hydra, Libra, and Serpens.

**Special Features:** This gigantic constellation is the second largest in the sky. The brightest object in Virgo is Spica, a blue-white star with an impressive magnitude of 1.0. Perhaps its best known feature is the "Virgo Cluster". Far more impressive than any star cluster, this is actually a cluster of eight galaxies! Included in these is the famous "Sombrero Galaxy". All of the galaxies are located close to the border of Coma Berenices. There is a well known double star in Virgo, known as Porrima. It consists of two yellow-white stars which orbit each other. Virgo is also home to three meteor showers on the 26th of March, and the 9th and 25th of April.

## VOLANS - THE FLYING FISH

**Quick Facts:** Volans was discovered by the Dutch Astronomers Frederick de Houtman and Pieter Dirkszoon Keyser between 1595-7.

**Visibility:** Not visible form Great Britain

**Location:** Volans is a Southern Hemisphere constellation, neighboured by Carina, Pictor, Dorado, Mensa, and Chameleon.

**Special Features:** Volans is an aesthetically pleasing constellation whose outline perhaps more closely mirrors a kite in flight, than a flying fish. The brightest object in the constellation are also the most interesting, a pair of double stars with magnitudes of 3.8 and 5.7.

## VULPECULA - THE FOX

**Background** Vulpecula, another Southern Hemisphere constellation, was discovered by the Johannes Hevelius in 1690.

**Visibility:** June - November

**Location:** Vulpecula is neighboured by Cygnus, Lyra,

Hercules, Sagitta, Delphinus, and Pegasus.

**Special Features:** Although Vulpecula is not very bright, there are still several interesting objects to discover in the constellation. The brightest of these is Alpha Velpeculae, a red giant with a magnitude of 4.4. Vulpecula may be best known, historically, as the sight of the discovery of the first pulsar in 1967. The most fantastic sight, however, is the beautiful nebula, known as "The Dumbbell".

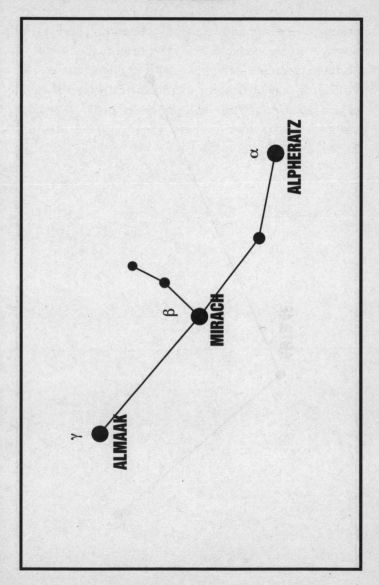

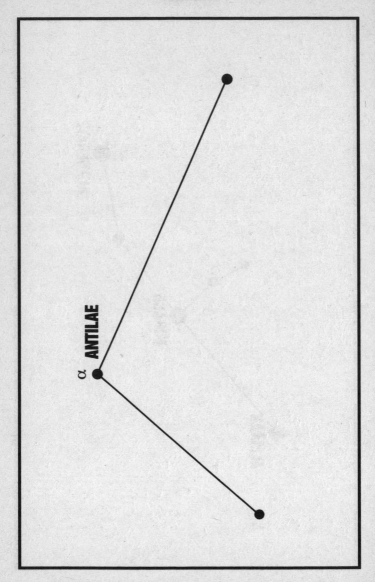

α ANTILAE

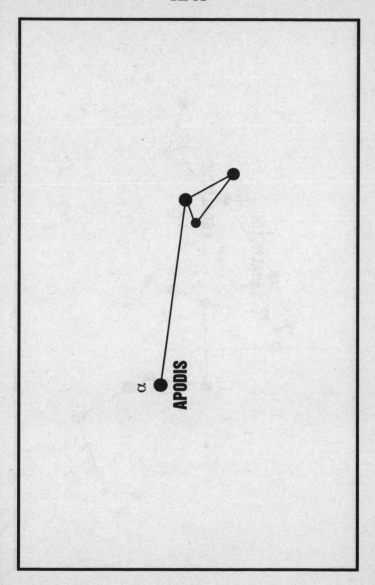

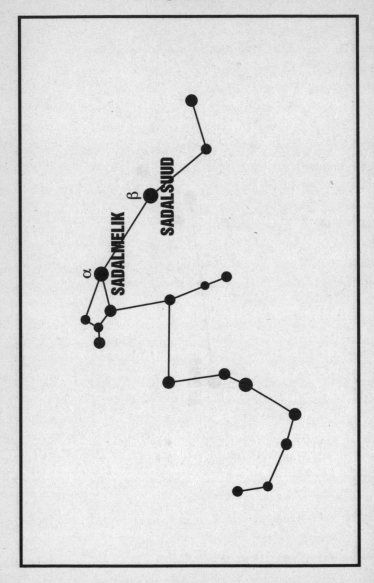

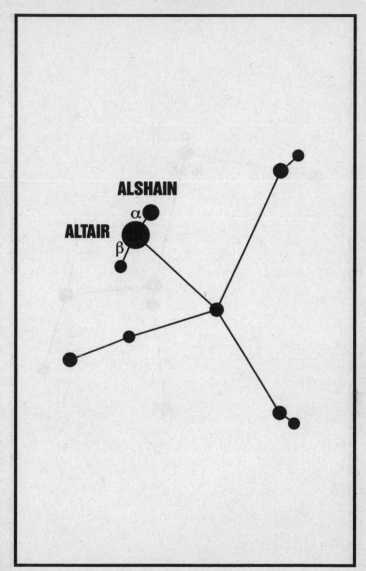

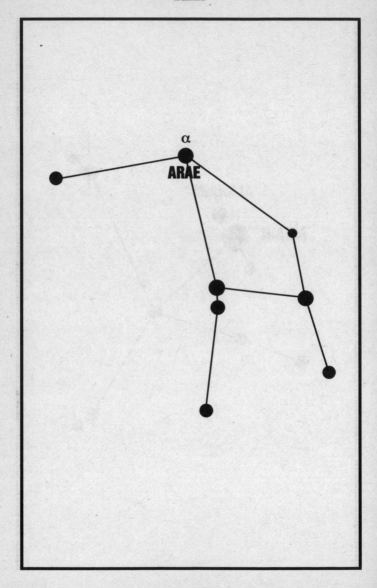

α

ARAE

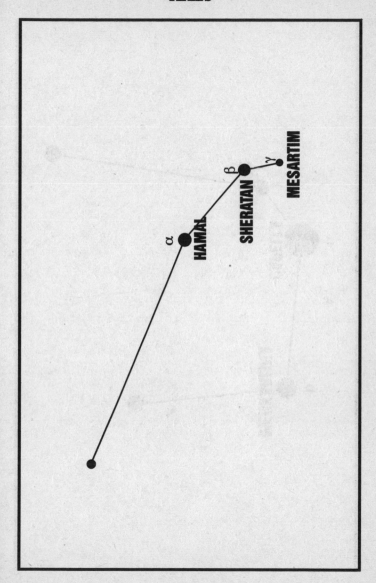

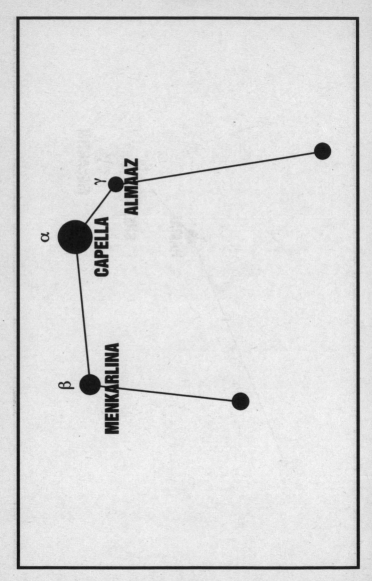

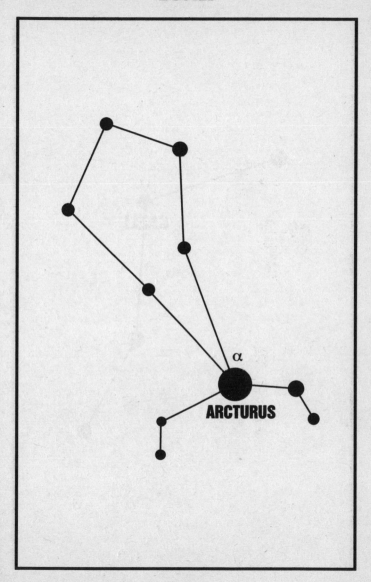

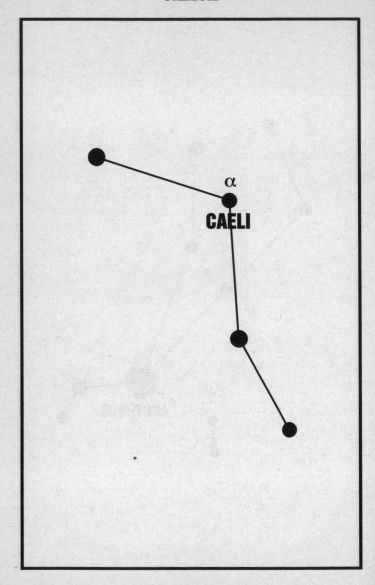

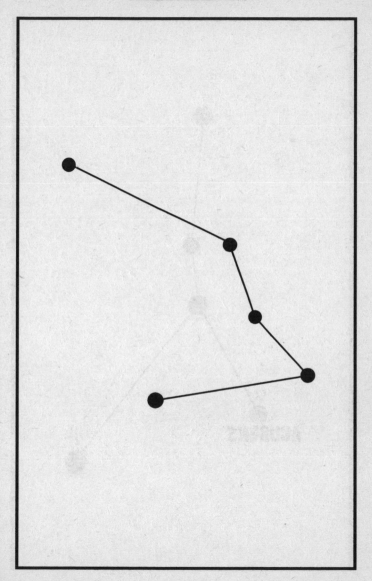

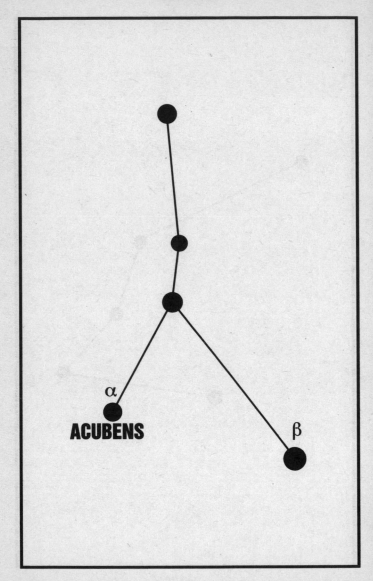

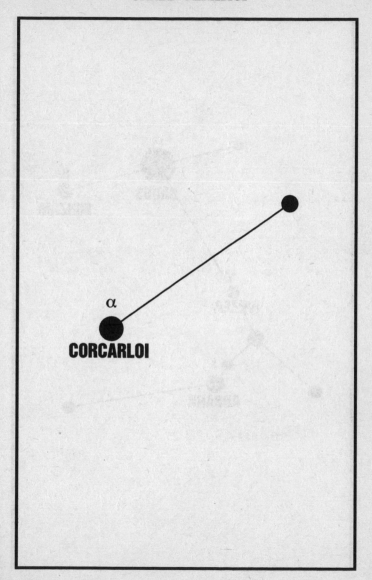

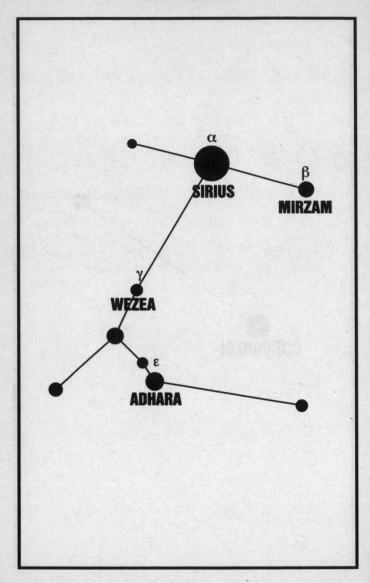

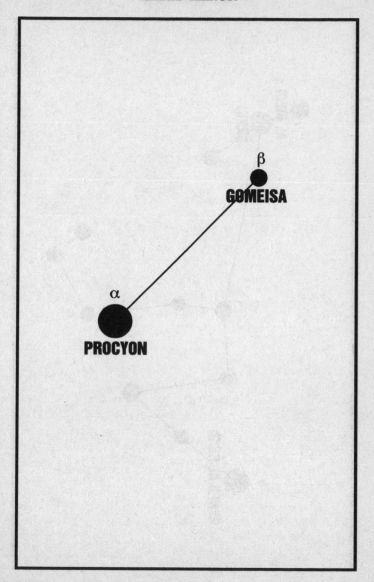

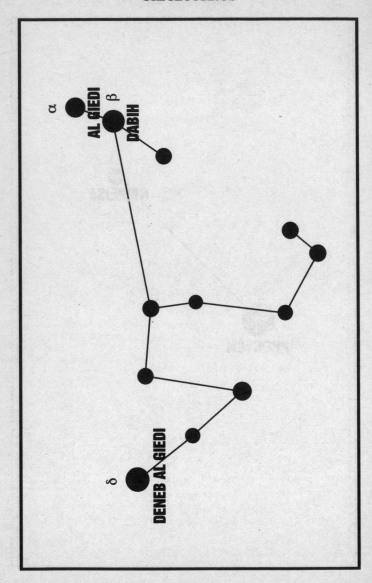

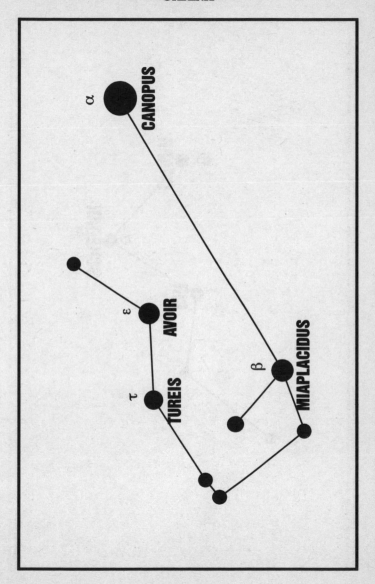

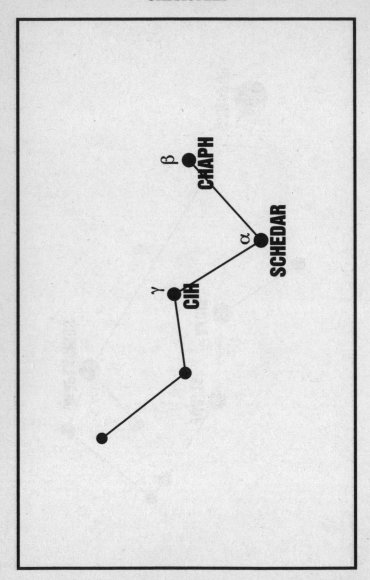

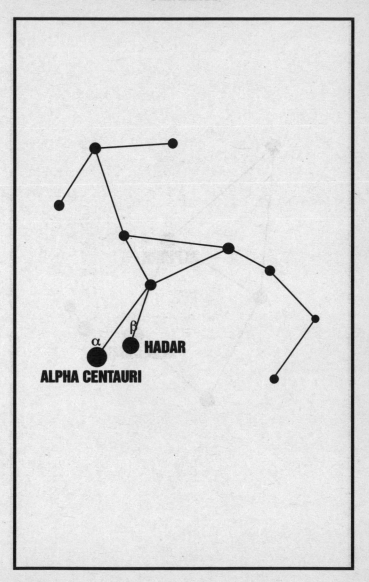

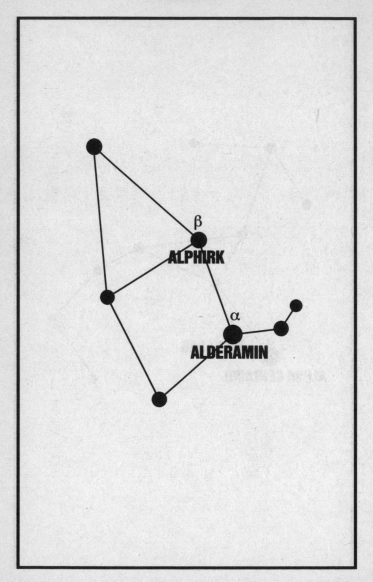

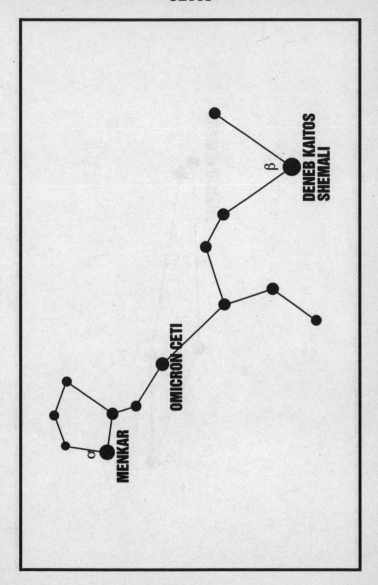

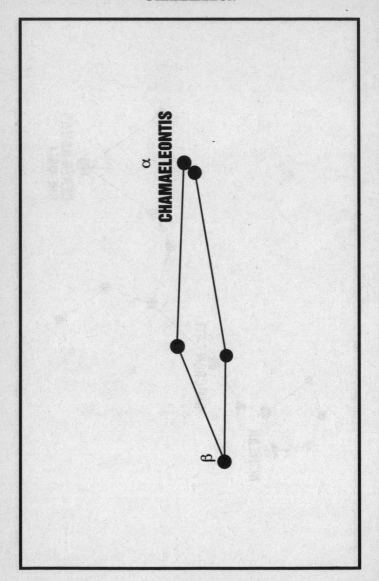

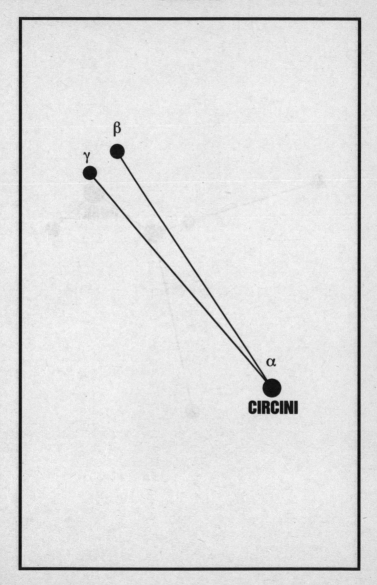

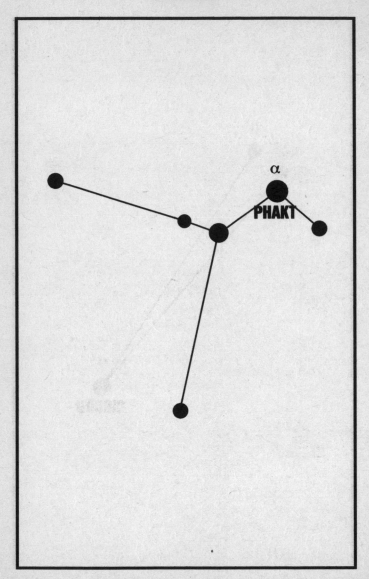

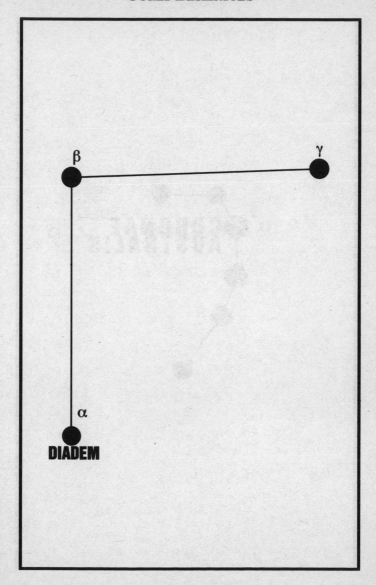

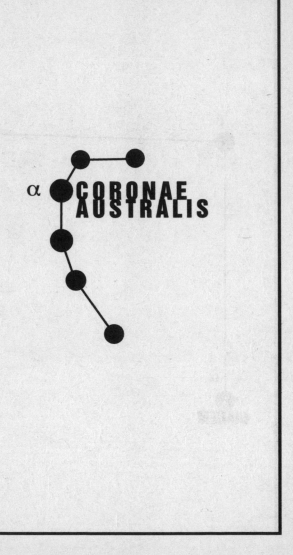

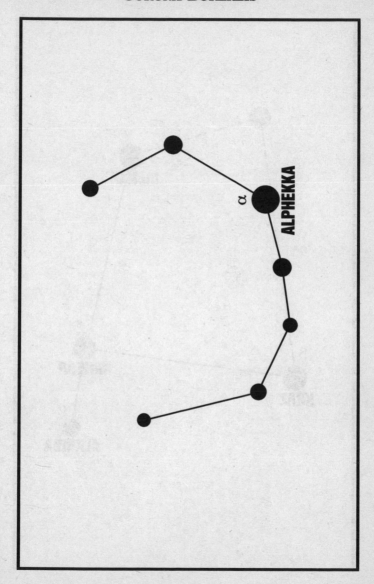

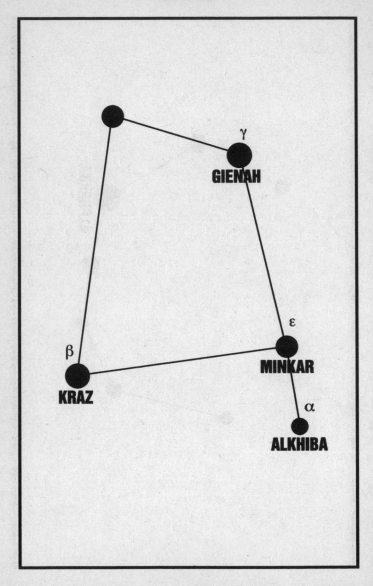

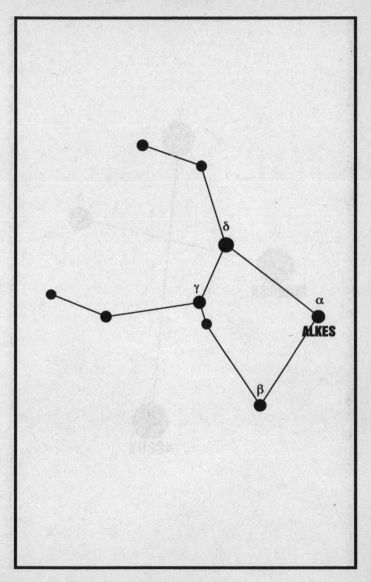

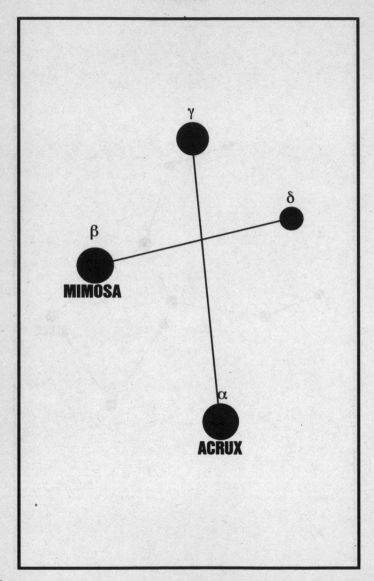

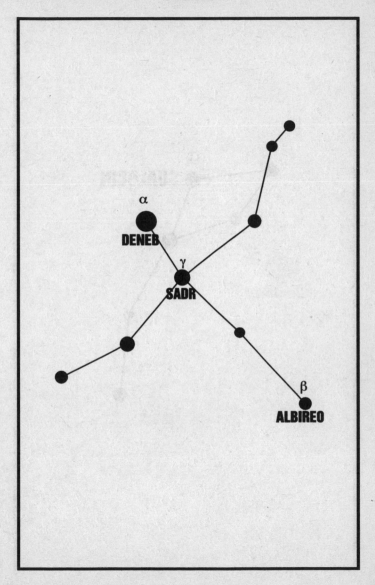

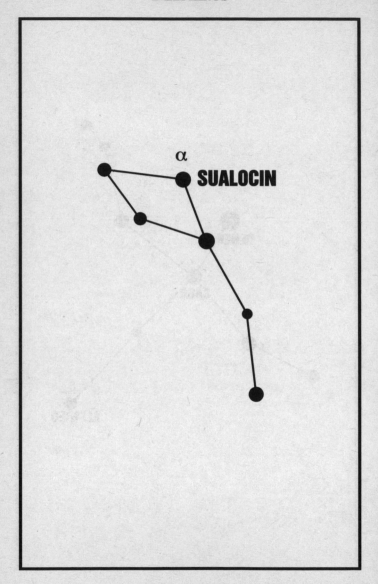

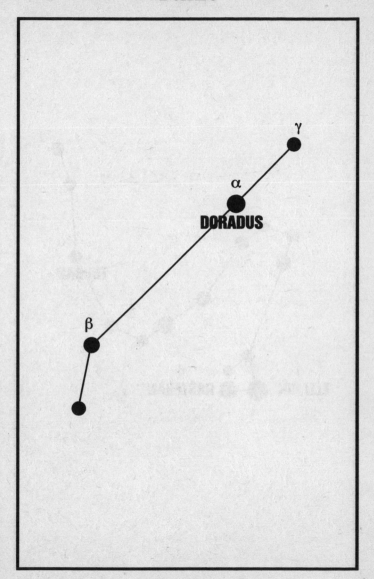

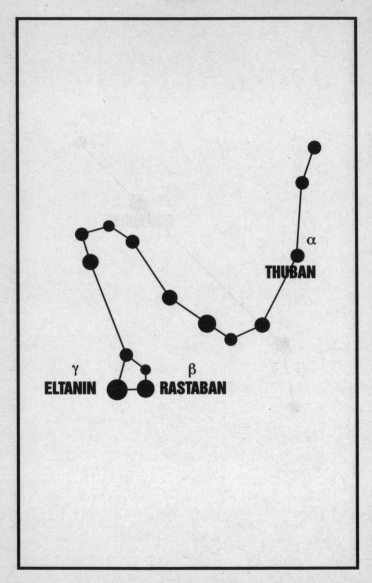

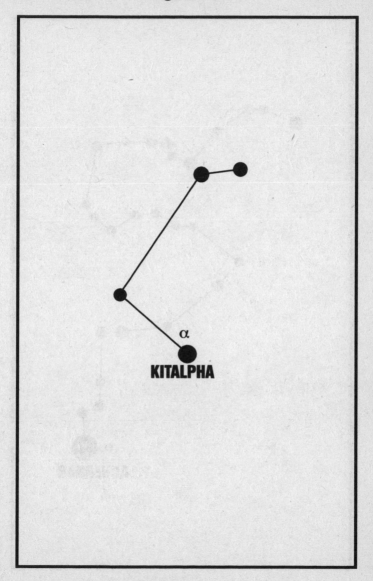

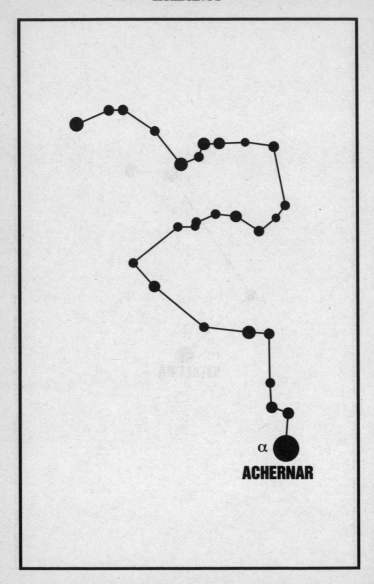

α
**ACHERNAR**

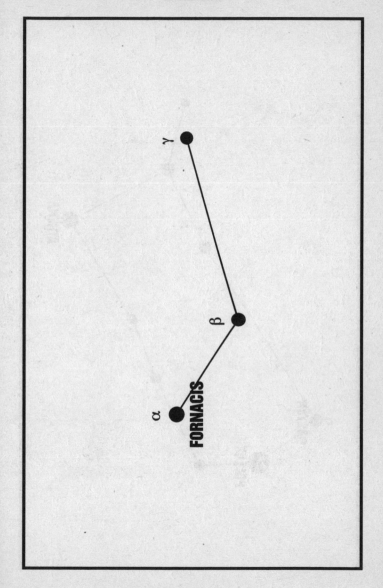

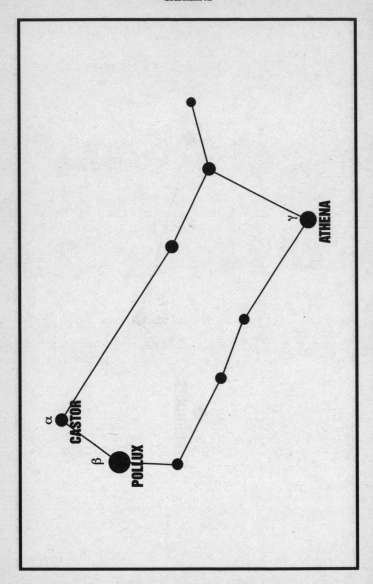

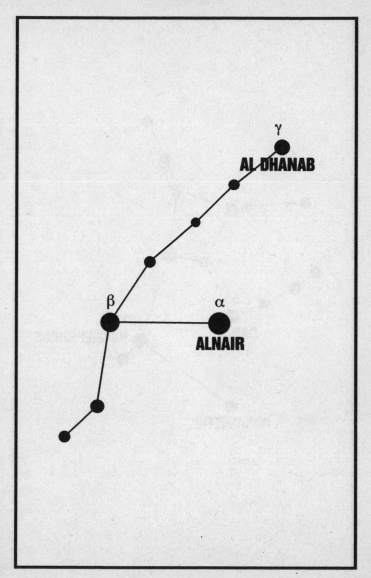

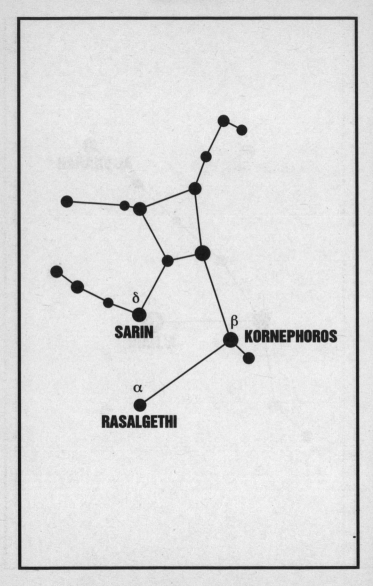

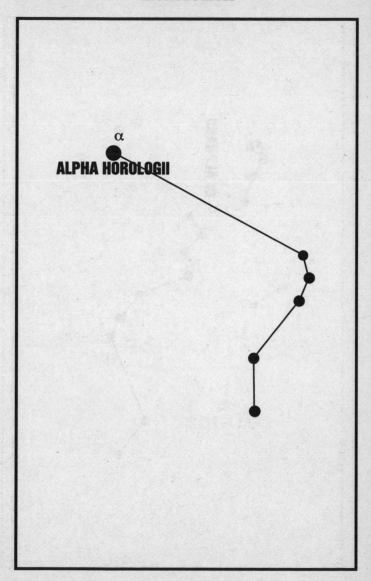

α

**ALPHA HOROLOGII**

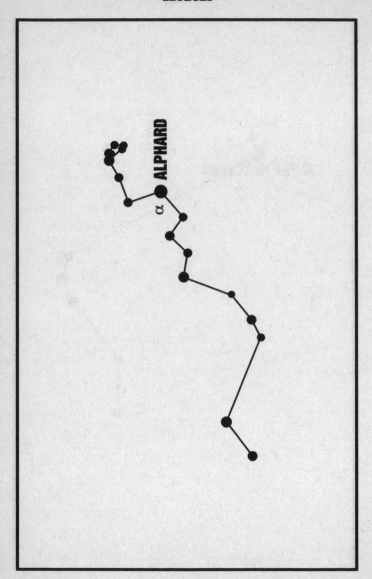

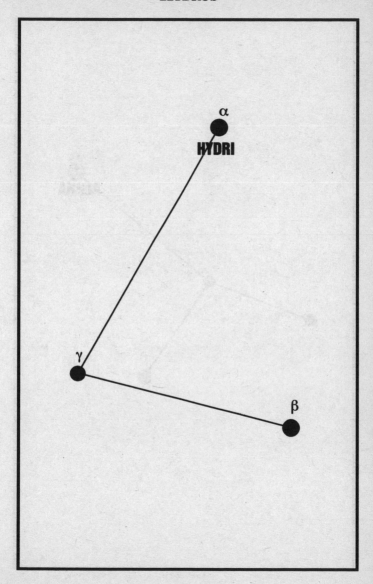

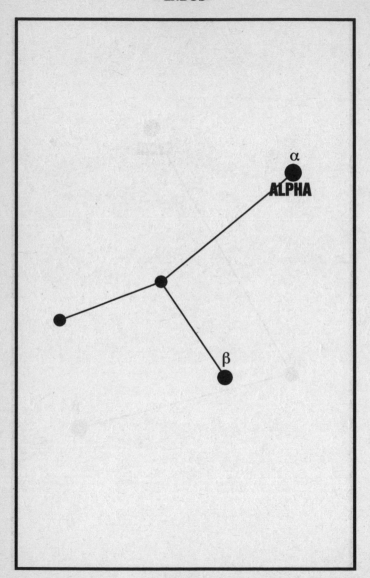

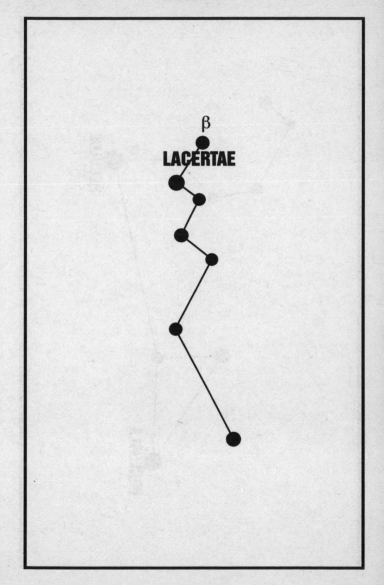

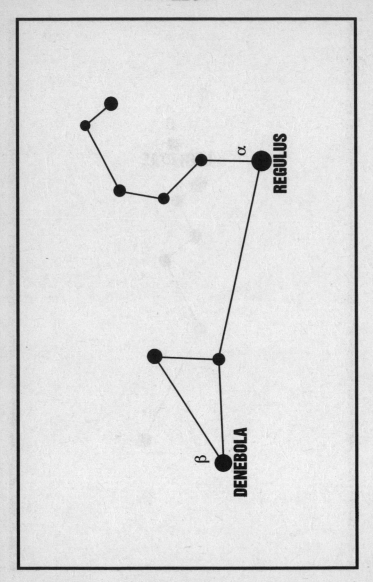

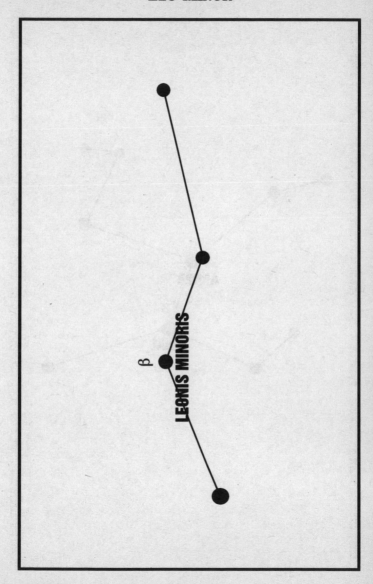

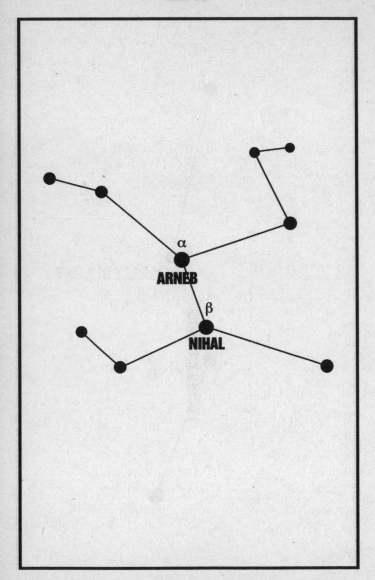

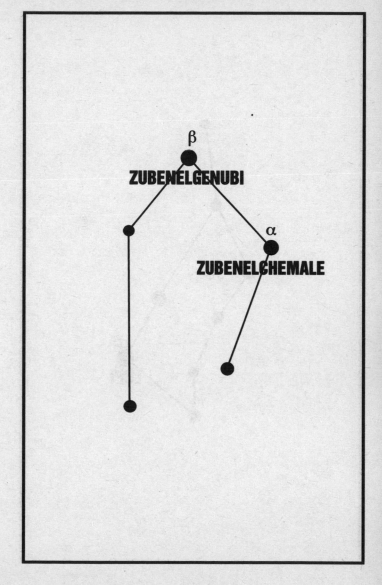

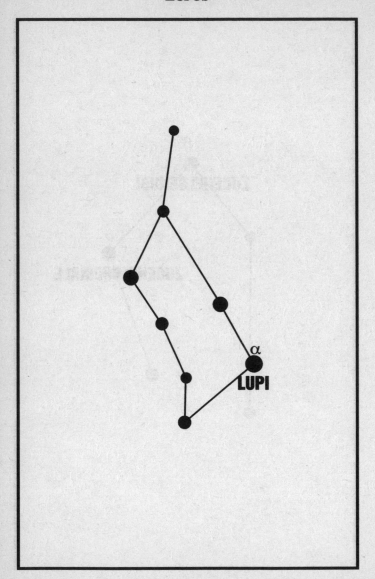

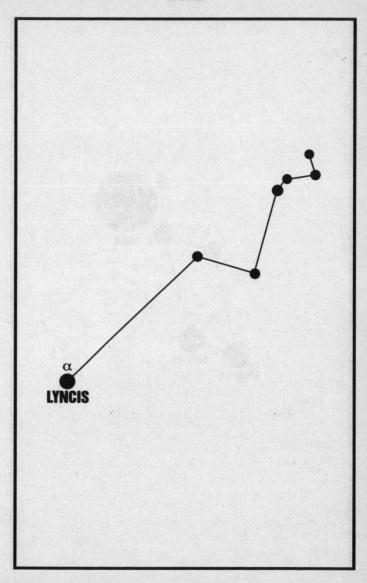

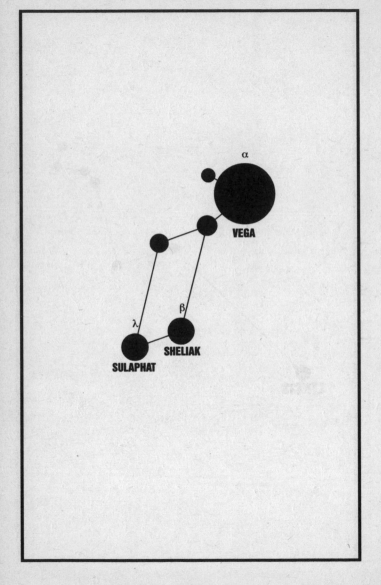

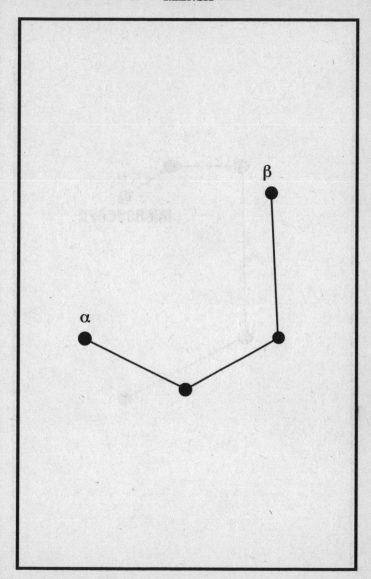

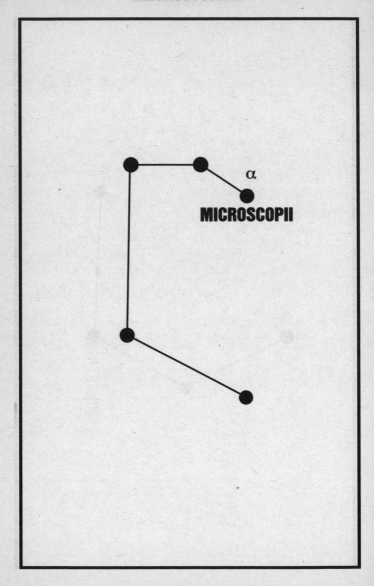

α

MICROSCOPII

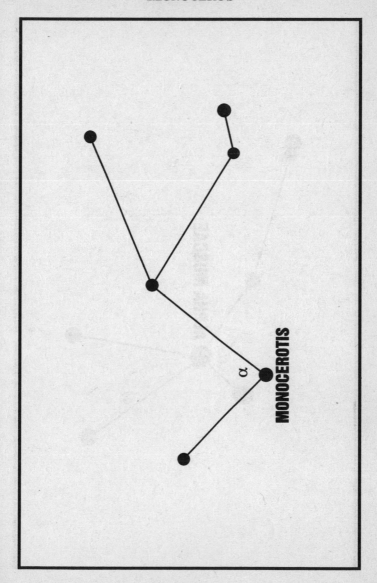

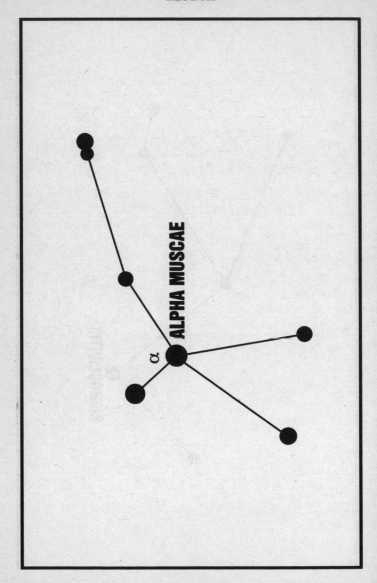

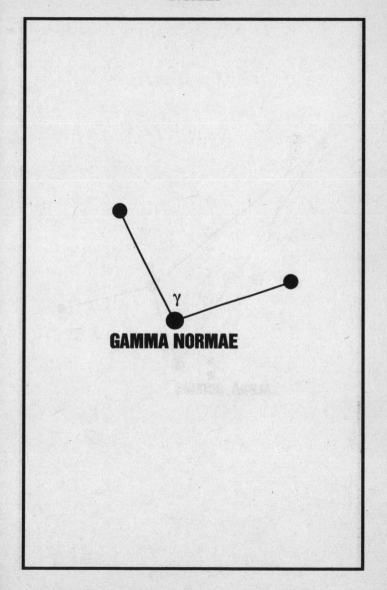

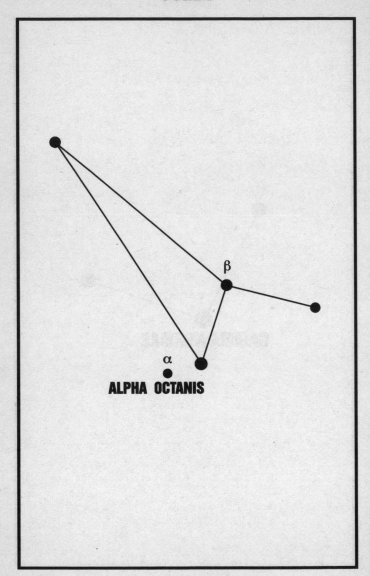

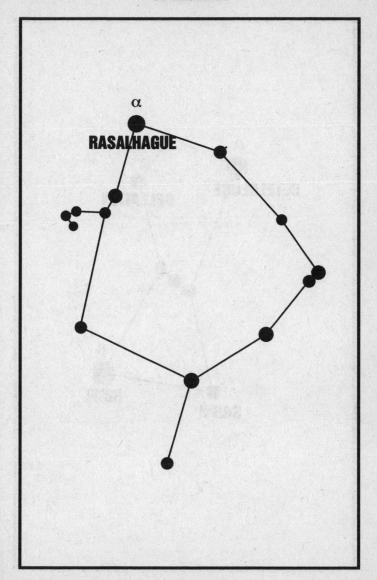

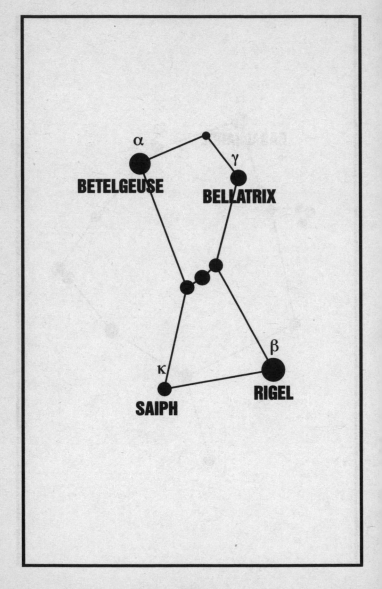

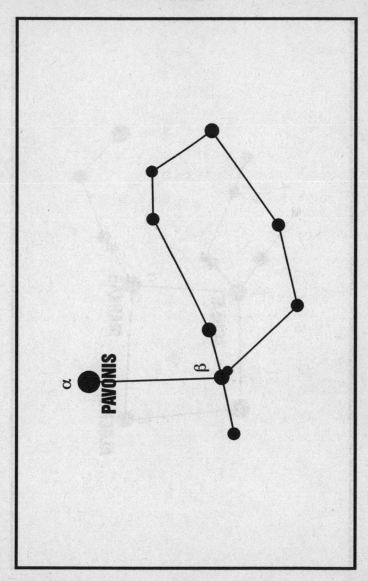

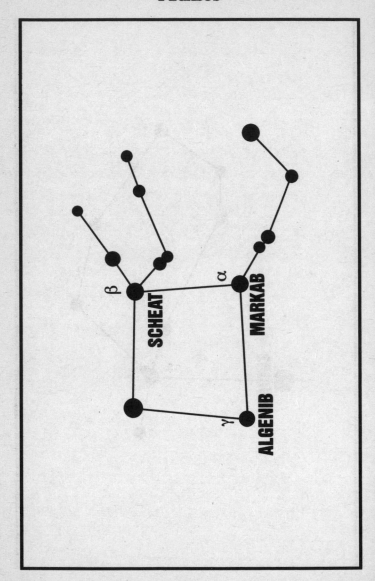

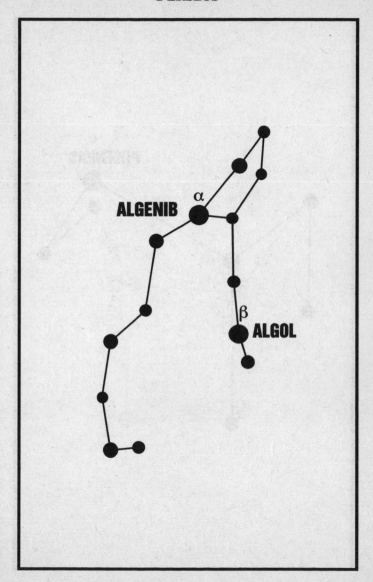

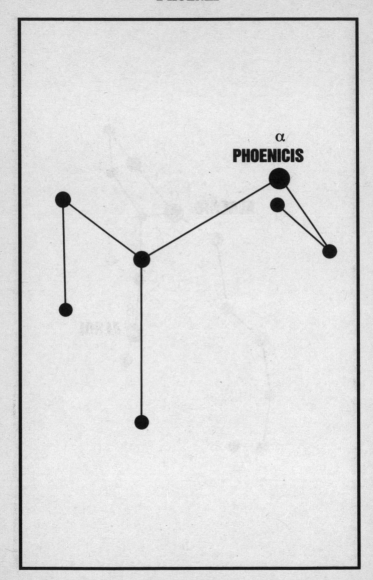

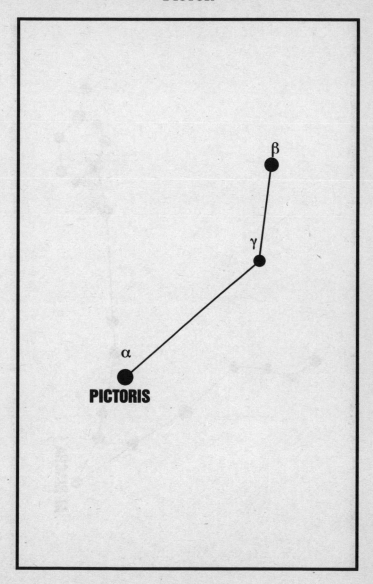

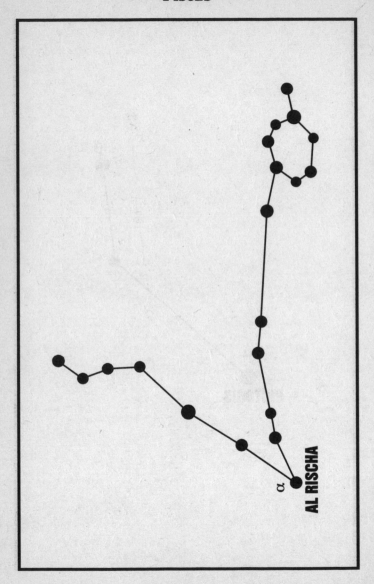

α

AL RISCHA

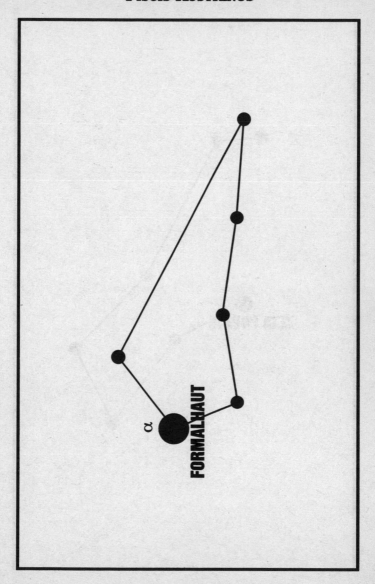

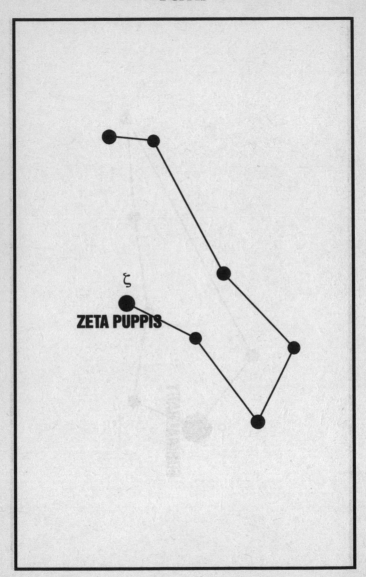

ζ

**ZETA PUPPIS**

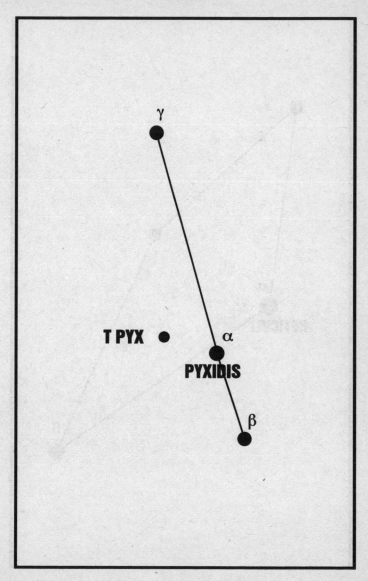

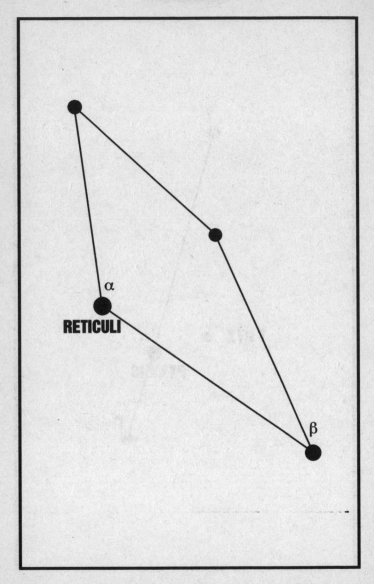

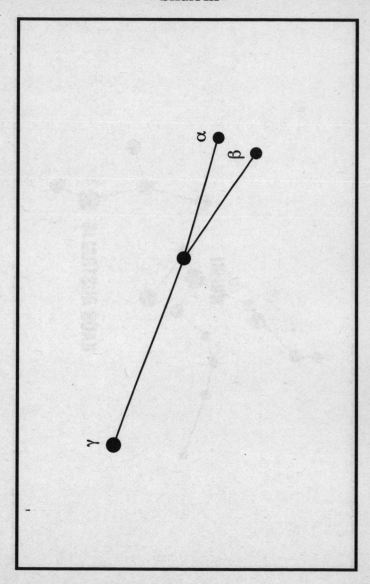

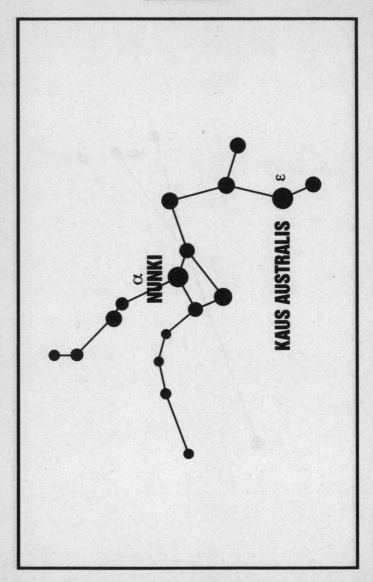

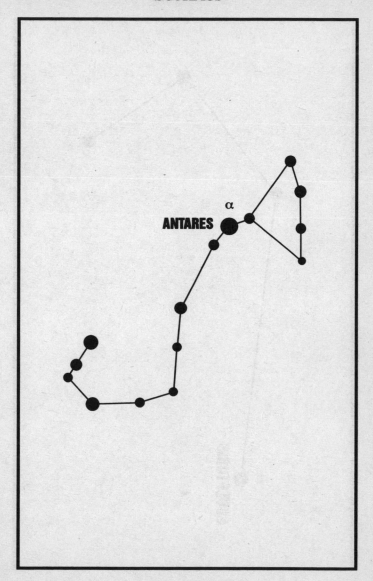

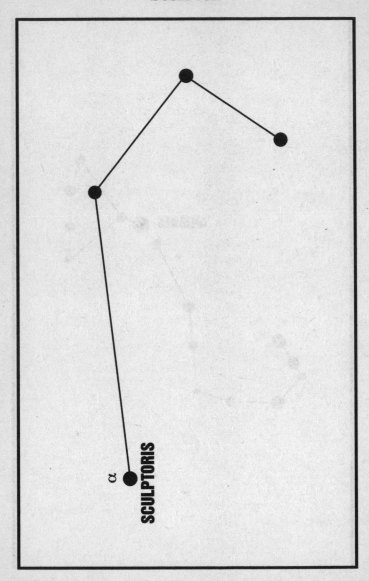

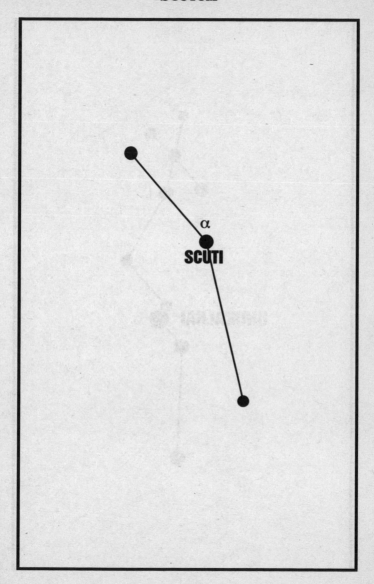

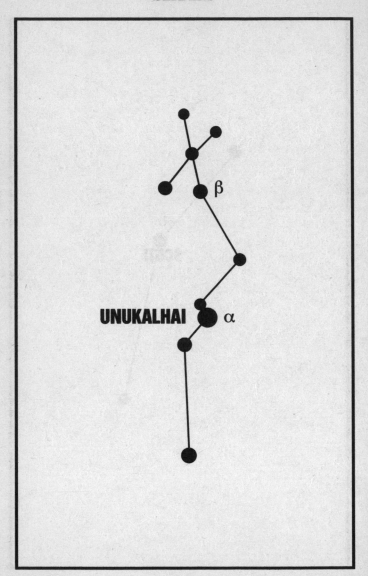

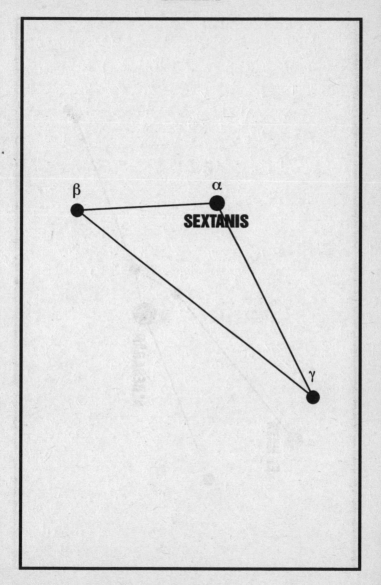

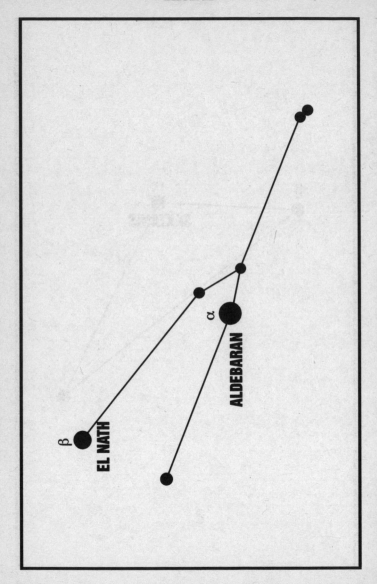

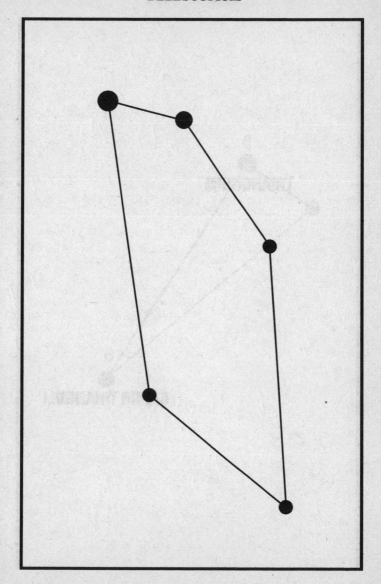

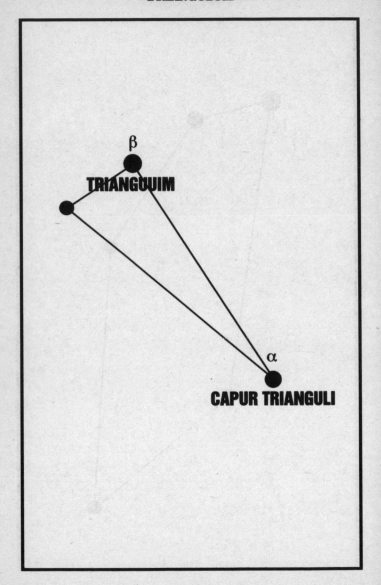

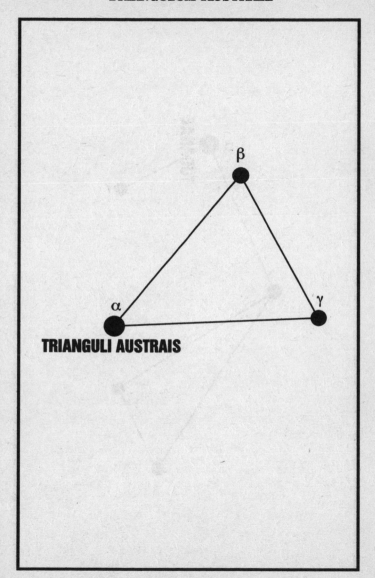

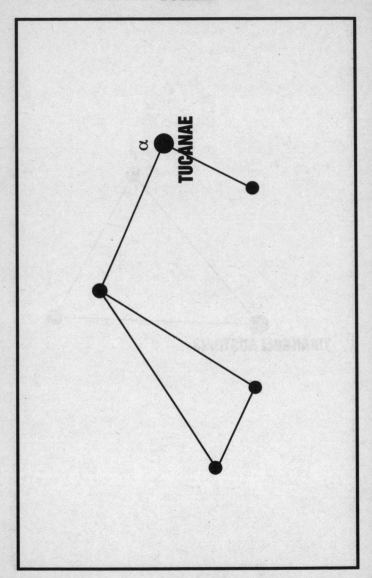

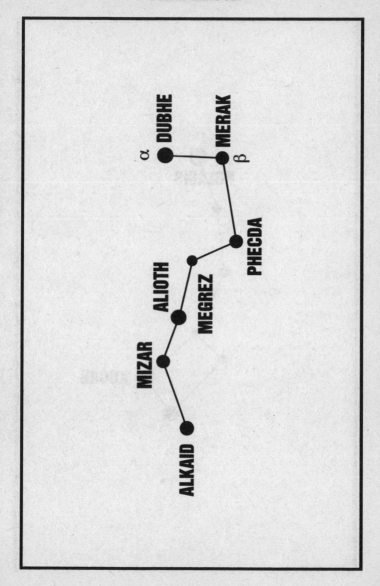

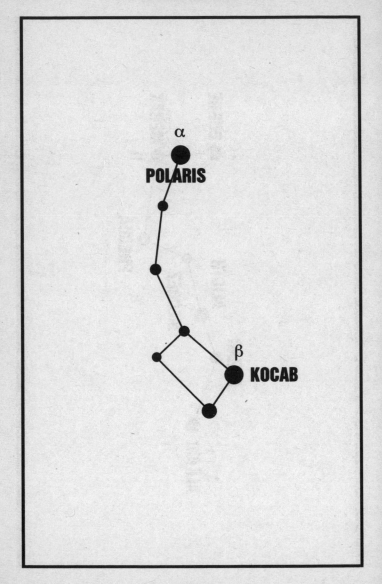

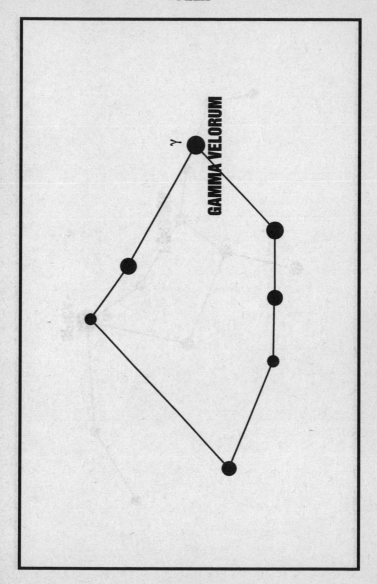

GAMMA VELORUM

γ

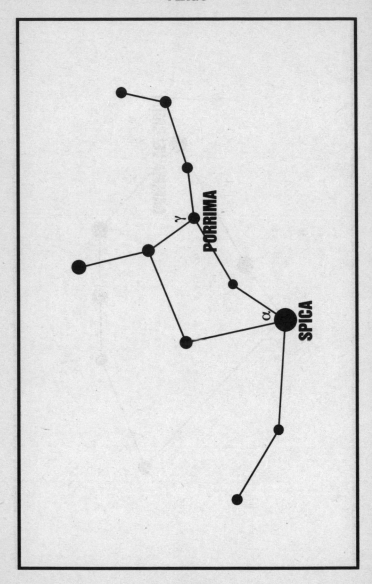

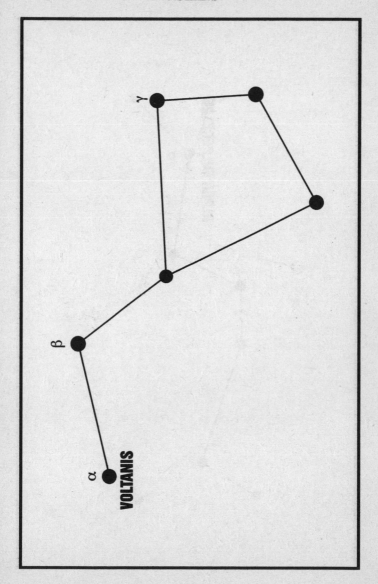

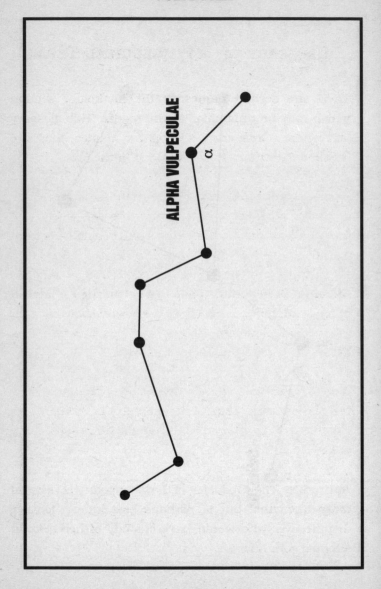

# GLOSSARY OF MYTHOLOGICAL TERMS

There are several names in the mythology section which may be unfamiliar to the reader. This glossary serves as a reference section for names that are mentioned, but not fully explained in the text.

**Aescupalis (Ophiuchus)** The first and greatest doctor in Greek mythology, he is known as the founder of medicine and had the ability to bring people back from the dead.

**Alcmene** A beautiful maiden who married a mortal named Amphitryon. She is best known for giving birth to Hercules. This came about after Zeus slept with her, by disguising himself as her husband.

**Amphitryon** The father (in name only) of Hercules. The real father was Zeus, but Amphitryon brought up Hercules as his own son and taught him some of the defensive arts.

**Aphrodite** The Goddess of Love appears in several different myths, but is perhaps best known for her dispute over who would have custody of her beloved adopted son, Adonis.

**Apollo** The son of Zeus and brother of Artemis, he was considered the God of Beauty. He was involved in several mythological adventures, one of which was slaying the Dragon known as Python.

**Ariadne** The beautiful princess of Crete, she is best known for saving Theseus from the Minotaur by secretly providing him with a sword and a spool of thread, so that he could find his way out of the Labyrinth. She eventually married the God Dionysus, and went to live in Olympus.

**Artemis** The daughter of Zeus and twin sister of Apollo, she was considered the Goddess of the Hunt. She is probably best known for turning the nymph Callisto into a bear.

**Athamas** King of Boetia and father of Phrixus and Helle. He is probably best known for being tricked by his deceitful wife into sacrificing his own children. They were saved at the last minute by divine intervention, as a golden ram flew them to safety.

**Athena** The Warrior Goddess, and the Goddess of Reason. She is mentioned several times in different myths. She acted as the benefactor of Hercules and Odysseus, and fought against the Titans. She is perhaps best known for her own birth, during which she sprung out of Zeus's head fully clothed in armour and ready for battle.

**Augias** A son of the Sun (Helios). He travelled with the Argonauts on their search for the Golden Fleece. He is best remembered for his stables, which had never been cleaned. It was one of Hercules' Twelve Labours to clean them, which he did by diverting two rivers through them.

**Argonauts** The name given to the fifty men who sailed with Jason in search of the Golden Fleece. Their adventure is one of the best known in all of Greek mythology, and the Argonauts themselves were made up of some of the greatest heroes of the time. They included, to name a few, Castor and Pollux (Gemini), Orpheus (Lyra), and Hercules

**Callisto** (Ursa Major) A wood-nymph and hunter, she spent her days with Artemis, Goddess of the Hunt. She is best known for being impregnated by Zeus and giving birth to Arcas (Bootes). She was turned into a bear by Artemis, who was jealous of her affection for Zeus.

**Carcinus** (Cancer) Carcinus was the name of the crab who bit Hercules' heel while he was in battle with the Hydra.

**Castor** Along with his brother Pollux, they made up the Dioscuri (Gemini). Both he and his brother travelled together, and were well known for their exploits with the Argonauts. Together, they figure prominently in several myths.

**Chiron** (Centaurus) The son of Cronus. He was a kindly Centaur, who tutored many of Greece's heroes, including Jason and Apollo. He was accidentally shot, and eventually killed, by one of Hercules' poisoned arrows.

**Cronus** The King of the Titans and one time ruler of Heaven and Earth. It was prophesised that his son would dethrone him, so he ate them all as soon as they were born. He forced his wife, Gaia (Mother Earth), to go into hiding the next time she was pregnant, and fooled Cronus into swallowing a rock instead of the child. That child was Zeus, who, of course, fulfilled the prophecy.

**Dionysus** The God of Wine and the Vine, his mystical and often excessive behaviour helped inspire his cult following on both sides of the Mediterranean. He is best known for introducing wine to man.

**Ericthonius** (Auriga) This half-man, half-serpent was one of the first Kings of Athens. He is best known for inventing the four horse chariot.

**Erigone** An Athenian maiden who married Dionysus, God of the Vine. She is best known as the daughter of Icarius, who received the gift of wine from Dionysus, and passed it on to mankind.

**Eros** The God of Love, he is often pictured as what we might know as Cupid, a small child with wings and an arrow, which would make their victims fall desperately in love.

**Euphemus** The son of Poseidon, he was a member of the Argonauts and is most famous for sending a dove (Columba) through the Symplegades (Clashing Rocks), and showing them the path to safety.

**Europa** The beautiful daughter of King Agenor, she is most famous for being seduced by Zeus when he disguised himself as a White Bull (Taurus), and carried her off to Crete, where she gave birth to three sons.

**Ganymede** (Aquarius) The son of King Tros, he was said to be the fairest youth in the world. He was taken to Olympus by Zeus and served as the cup-bearer to the Gods.

**Hephaestus** The God of Fire and Metals. He was the son of Zeus and Hera, and is best known for his battles with the Titans, and his exploits in the Trojan War.

**Hera** The Queen of the Gods. She married Zeus, and is mentioned in hundreds of myths. She is best known for her acts of vengeance on the numerous lovers of her philandering husband.

**Hercules** The greatest Greek hero. He was the son of Zeus and as a result, was stronger than any mortal man. His exploits are far too many to mention, but he is best known for his legendary "Twelve Labours".

**Hesperides** The Hesperides were three maidens who were best known as the care-takers of the Garden of the Gods. Their main responsibility was to guard Hera's golden apple tree, along with Draco the dragon.

**Hind of Ceryneia** This legendary animal was known for its tremendous horns and great speed. Hercules' fourth labour was to kill the animal. Hercules chased it for a year, before finally wounding it with an arrow and slowing it down.

**Idas** Considered to be the mightiest and bravest of mortal men. He is best known for his exploits with Jason and the Argonauts, and his fatal battle with Castor and Pollux.

**Medusa** The most famous of the three Gorgons. Once a beautiful maiden, she was transformed into a horrible monster by Hera, who was jealous of her. She had snakes for hair, and if anyone saw her face they would turn to stone. She was eventually beheaded by the hero Perseus.

**Minotaur** A horrible half-man half-bull. It lived in a labyrinth, and devoured fourteen sacrificial victims every year, until he was eventually killed by Theseus, with the help of Ariadne.

**Nemean Lion** A monstrous cave lion. He terrorised, and devoured the inhabitants of Nemea. He was eventually killed by Hercules, who took his pelt, and used it as an impenetrable shield.

**Nereids** A group of fifty sea nymphs who lived with Poseidon. They were known for their beauty and grace.

**Olympus** The mountain home of the Gods

**Oracle of Ammon** A famous oracle, located in Egypt, that prophesised several mythological events most notably that Cepheus would have to offer his daughter, Andromeda, as a sacrifice to Cetus the sea-monster. Like many prophecies in ancient mythology, it came true with a spin on the story. Andromeda did not have to die for Cetus to be done away with, just offered as a sacrifice.

**Orion** The greatest hunter in Greek Mythology. He was a giant, incredibly strong and handsome, and had the ability to walk on water. He is most famous for ridding the island Chios of all its beasts, in a failed attempt to win the hand of Merope.

**Orpheus** The greatest of all musicians. His music was so beautiful that it could charm any living being. He is most famous for his part in the search for the Golden Fleece, and his failed attempt to save his wife from the Underworld.

**Pan** An anomaly amongst the Gods, this half-man half-goat was quite content not to live in Olympus with the rest of the gods. He preferred to frolic or sleep in the shade of the trees, playing his flute, and seducing the wood nymphs. He is the only God to ever die. Not surprisingly, he still has a cult following today.

**Persephone** The daughter of Zeus and Demeter. She was the Goddess of the Underworld, and wife of Hades. She is best known for being abducted by Hades and taken into the Underworld. She was also part-time mother to Adonis.

**Perseus** One of the greatest Greek heroes, he is known for several acts of bravery. He is probably most famous for beheading Medusa, and saving the Princess Andromeda.

**Phaetheon** The son of Helios (The Sun) who begged his father to let him ride his sun chariot on its route across the sky. Tragically, he lost control and, eventually, Zeus had to shoot him down with a thunderbolt, or risk the Sun crashing in to the Earth.

**Pholus** One of the few friendly centaurs, he is best known for serving Hercules wine, which was only meant to be consumed communally by the centaurs. When the other centaurs smelled the wine they attacked Hercules, and Pholus was accidentally killed.

**Phrixus and Helle** were meant to be sacrificed by their father, King Athamas, who was tricked into doing so by his jealous second wife, Ino. They were saved by Zeus, who sent down a golden fleeced ram that picked them up and flew them off to safety.

**Pollux** Twin brother of Castor, who together made up the Discuri (Gemini). Pollux was a great boxer, but was best known for his adventures with his brother, particularly while sailing with Jason and the Argonauts.

**Polydectes** The evil ruler of a small island, on which Perseus and his mother sought refuge. He attempted to get Perseus killed by sending him on a mission to behead Medusa, but paid with his own life when Perseus triumphantly returned to discover that Polydectes had tried to abduct his mother in his absence.

**Poseidon** The God of the Sea and brother to Zeus, he possessed an often bitter and angry nature. He is known for his trident and his sea chariot, led by giant sea-horses. He was noted for his tendency to conjure up Sea monsters that would terrorise mortals.

**Prometheus** The cousin of Zeus, who gave fire to man. He is perhaps best known for accepting Chiron's (Sagittarius) immortality, so that the suffering Centaur could be allowed to die.

**Semele** The mother of the God Dionysus, and one of Zeus's many lovers. She was tragically killed when Zeus revealed himself to her in his true form, and she was struck down by one of the thunderbolts that surrounded his body.

**Stymphalian Birds** Giant birds of prey with steel feathers and claws. They were said to be able to swallow a man whole. They were killed by Hercules as one of his "Twelve Labours".

**Theseus** King of Athens, and one of the greatest Greek heroes, he is probably best known for killing the Minotaur and freeing the Athenians from Crete.

**Titans** The Titans were a group of Giants and monsters who ruled the Earth before the Gods. The Gods fought an epic battle with them, and eventually took control of heaven and Earth.

**Tros** Trojan hero and King, perhaps most famous as the father of Ganymede (Aquarius).

**Typhon** A hideous monster, half-man half-serpent, whose mission it was to kill the Gods as vengeance for

their defeat of the Titans.

**Zeus** The all-powerful King of Gods. Zeus is by far the most mentioned character in Greek mythology. He is perhaps best known for changing his form in order to secretly seduce scores of unsuspecting Goddesses and maidens. Despite his rather self serving character, he was considered to be fairer, and more forgiving, than many of the other gods.

---